The Mysteries of Plant Life

AGS

by
Paula Tedford Diaco

AGS®

American Guidance Service, Inc.
4201 Woodland Road
Circle Pines, MN 55014-1796
1-800-328-2560

Experiences in Science

Printed in the United States of America

ISBN 0–7854–0972–6 (Previously ISBN 0–88671–957–7)

Order Number: 90893

A 0 9 8 7 6 5 4

Contents

The Kingdoms of Living Things

Many living organisms exist in the world. They can be divided into five kingdoms: protists, monerans, fungi, plants, and animals. Each kingdom is made up of a large group of organisms that resemble one another or that share similar traits. Studying the kingdoms helps scientists understand how living things are related to one another.

Bacteria are one of the oldest and simplest life forms. Plants may have evolved from bacteria. Many animals eat plants to survive and so live where plants grow. The most complex living things are the members of the animal kingdom.

The simplest form of any living thing is a cell, a tiny grouping of living material. The more advanced a living thing is, the more cells it contains. The cells become more specialized and complex. Plants and animals are grouped according to how simple or how complex they are.

Euglena are microscopic organisms. Notice the eyespot and the flagellum on the *Euglena* in the illustration.

If you see a squirrel sitting in an oak tree, it is easy to tell the animal from the plant. However, primitive plants and animals are often harder to separate. Some have traits that make them appear to be both plants and animals.

Primitive *Euglena* are microscopic; they can be seen only with the aid of a microscope. The green "soup" that often grows on the surface of ponds and lakes is made up of *Euglena.* Like plants, they contain **chloroplasts,** small green objects that use light energy to produce food. In addition, they have tails, called **flagella** (singular: *flagellum*), that help them move around in the water. They also have an eyespot. It is not like a human eye, but it is light sensitive. It helps *Euglena* know where they are. *Euglena,* then, are a little like a plant and a little like an animal.

Scientists who study animals are called *zoologists.* Scientists who study plants are called *botanists.* They study the shapes of plants, the parts that make up a plant, and how a plant grows from a seed to a full-grown plant. Botanists use specialized terms to describe plants. Key terms are included in the glossary at the end of the book. Refer to this glossary frequently as you study each unit.

███ Write the answers to the following questions.

1. What are the five kingdoms of living things? _____

2. What is a cell? _____

3. What are *Euglena?* _____

4. What are chloroplasts? _____

5. What is an eyespot? _____

Bacteria

Bacteria (singular: *bacterium*) are one of the five groups of living things. They are the most abundant life forms on earth. Bacteria have existed since ancient times and can be found in the earliest fossils. Because they share some traits with plants, they were considered plants until recently.

Bacteriologists (scientists who study bacteria) now consider bacteria to be a separate group of living things because their cells are simpler and more primitive than those of plants. Their cells reproduce differently from plant cells, too.

Bacteria are among the smallest living organisms. They live as single cells or as groups of cells clumped together. A microscope is needed to see a single bacterial cell. Bacteria come in four shapes: **vibrios, cocci, bacilli**, and **spirilla**. These shapes can be seen in the illustrations.

Although they are called *primitive,* bacteria are very **diverse** and do many things. Some types of bacteria are helpful; others are harmful. Bacteria help make foods, such as vinegar, cheese, and sauerkraut. Many helpful bacteria also break down and **decompose** dead matter, such as dead leaves and trees. The decomposed leaves and trees become part of soil. Bacteria are used in sewage treatment plants because they are very good at breaking down raw sewage into less harmful forms. Harmful bacteria can cause sickness, such as sore throats, infections, and pneumonia. There are many more types of helpful bacteria than harmful bacteria.

Read the following statements. If the statement is true, write *True* on the line provided. If the statement is not true, write *False.*

_____ 1. Bacteria are abundant.

_____ 2. Bacteria used to be called plants.

_____ 3. Bacteria are the largest living organisms.

_____ 4. Bacteria are used to make food such as cheese and sauerkraut.

_____ 5. All bacteria are harmful because they cause sickness.

_____ 6. Some bacteria break down and decompose dead matter.

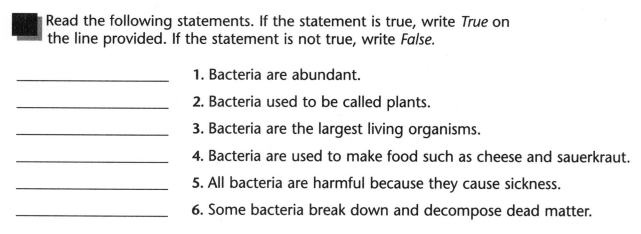

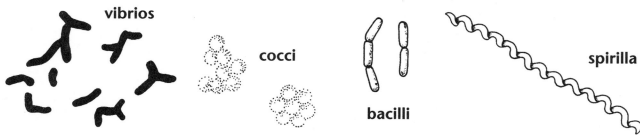

Bacteria are microscopic organisms that have four different shapes: *vibrios, cocci, bacilli,* and *spirilla.* In the illustrations, each shape is shown as it would appear under a microscope.

Parts of a Plant

Plants are made of cells. A cell is the smallest unit of a plant. From a single cell, a whole plant can grow. A single plant cell, just like a bacterial cell, is microscopic. Each plant is made up of thousands of cells. These cells form the roots, stems, and leaves.

Every plant cell is made up of many parts, called **organelles.** One of the most important organelles is the nucleus (plural: *nuclei*). It includes the plant's genetic material. These genes give plants specific traits. Some traits determine a plant's size or the color of its leaves and flowers. Genes make a plant look the way it does. All plants **inherit** genes, and therefore traits, from one or both parent plants. For instance, a red carnation can be crossed with a white carnation. The **offspring** in the first generation would be pink. The next generation would have pink, red, or white flowers. The offspring's color is a shared trait from both parent plants.

In plant cells, the nucleus is surrounded by a membrane, or a circle of protein. Bacterial cells do not have nuclei. This is one of the biggest differences between plants and bacteria.

Plant cells with the same function are usually found in the same place on a plant. Such groups of cells are called *tissues.* Each plant tissue has a specific function. Some tissues are roots, some are stems, and others make up the leaves. Roots, stems, and leaves are the three main parts of a plant.

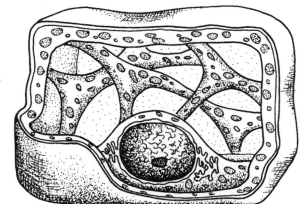

A cell wall surrounds each plant cell. The circular nucleus of the cell contains genes, or genetic material.

 Complete the following sentences. Write your answers on the lines provided.

1. Plants are made of _____.

2. A single plant cell is _____.

3. A single plant is made up of _____ of cells.

4. The various parts of a cell are called _____.

5. A group of cells with the same function is called _____.

6. A _____ is used to look at plant cells.

7. A _____ surrounds the nucleus of a plant cell.

8. A _____ cell does not have a nucleus.

9. The three main parts of a plant are the _____.

10. Roots, stems, and leaves are examples of a plant's _____.

Plants grow well in all kinds of **climates.** They use their roots, stems, and leaves to collect water, minerals, and gases. They use these things to make food and to stay alive.

Roots are buried underground for several reasons. First, roots hold the plants in place. They also collect water and minerals from the soil. Some plants have roots that store food. Carrots, sugar beets, and sweet potatoes are really the roots of certain vegetable plants. These roots contain sugar, minerals, and water. They store this food for the rest of the plant above the ground.

From the roots, plant stems grow above the ground. Stems carry plant food, water, and minerals throughout the plant. Stems also support plants. The leaves grow outward from the stems of the plants.

Leaves are the food factories for plants. Photosynthesis takes place in the plants' leaves. **Photosynthesis** is a chemical process that plants use to make sugar, their food. The plants take water and minerals from the soil and **carbon dioxide** from the air to produce sugar. Some plants—like the carrots, sugar beets, and sweet potatoes mentioned before—store their food. Plants store food as starch, a substance similar to sugar. Taste is one major difference between starch and sugar. Sugar is sweet; starch is not.

These three major parts of plants are very important. With their roots, stems, and leaves, plants are able to grow and make food.

A Match the sentence parts by writing the letter on the line provided.

_____ 1. Roots   a. as starch, a substance similar to sugar.

_____ 2. Stems   b. are the food factories of plants.

_____ 3. Leaves   c. are buried underground.

_____ 4. Plants store food   d. carry plant food, water, and minerals throughout the plant.

B Read each statement. If the statement is true, write *True* on the line provided. If it is not true, write *False.*

_____ 1. Plants grow in only a few climates.

_____ 2. Roots collect water and minerals from the soil.

_____ 3. Leaves grow outward from the roots of plants.

_____ 4. Carrots store food in their roots.

_____ 5. Photosynthesis is the chemical process that plants use to make food.

_____ 6. People eat the roots of sweet potato plants.

Plant Types

Plants are very diverse. They come in all sizes, shapes, and colors. Botanists take a scientific look at plants. They then classify plants that have seeds into one of two groups: **angiosperms** or **gymnosperms.**

Angiosperms and gymnosperms are the most easily recognized types of plants. Angiosperms are plants that produce and store their seeds in an **ovary,** or protective seed case. Examples include roses, elm trees, geraniums, and orchids. Gymnosperms are also easy to identify; these plants expose their seeds in a cone. Some examples of gymnosperms are pine, spruce, and redwood trees. You will learn more about these two groups in Unit 4.

Plants that have seeds are well developed and advanced. Many other kinds of plants do not produce seeds. These less developed plant types include mosses and ferns. They are considered primitive plants. You will learn more about these plants in Units 2 and 3.

Thousands of different plants are included in each of these three groups: angiosperms, gymnosperms, and primitive plants. Because so many plants exist, every plant in the world has been given its own scientific name. Botanists use the Latin language to name plants. For example, the Latin name for a coconut is *Cocos nucifera.* Every botanist in the world who studies coconuts calls them by this Latin name.

Using Latin gives scientists a common language. Giving a plant an official Latin name tells everyone which plant is being referred to. For instance, the European white lily has over 200 names in four different languages. When botanists want other botanists to know that they are talking about the European white lily, they call it by its Latin name, *Nymphaea alba.* The second Latin word names the plant's species and usually describes a characteristic of the plant. In this case, *alba* means "white." The Latin name is always put in italics to show that it is the scientific name for the plant.

Write the answers to the following questions.

1. What do botanists do? _____

2. What are three examples of angiosperms? _____

3. What are three examples of gymnosperms? _____

4. What are two examples of less developed plants? _____

5. What language is used to name plants? _____

6. How many names in different languages does the European white lily have? _____

7. Into what two groups are plants that have seeds divided? _____

8. What is the Latin name for a coconut? _____

9. What does the Latin species name usually describe? _____

How Long Plants Live

Plants not only have variety and diversity; they also live different lengths of time. Even plants that are classified in the same group can live different lengths of time. It depends on where the plants live and the conditions under which they grow.

The amount of time that plants are alive is called their life span. Once plants have started to grow and develop, their environment and their life span determine how long they live. The environment of plants includes temperature, amount of water, minerals in the soil, and presence or absence of **parasites.** However, even if the environment is kind, plants do not live forever.

Plants are divided into three groups according to their expected life span. Plants that are **annuals** grow for a single season only. They produce seeds and then die. Petunias, for example, are annuals. **Biennials** grow for two seasons. During the second season, they produce seeds and then die. Sweet William is a biennial. **Perennial** plants grow for several years. They produce seeds every year after the first few years.

Chrysanthemums, as well as many houseplants, are perennials. Some perennials can live to be hundreds or even thousands of years old. For example, trees are usually perennials. The giant sequoias (see Unit 4) in California are some of the oldest living perennial plants on our planet.

A Complete the following sentences. Write your answers on the lines provided.

1. The amount of time a plant is alive is called its _____.

2. Plants that are annuals grow for _____.

3. Biennials grow for _____.

4. Perennial plants grow for _____.

5. Some perennials can live to be _____ of years old.

6. The environment of plants includes _____, _____, _____, and _____.

B Underline the word or phrase that completes each sentence correctly.

1. Plants that are classified in the same group can live (longer, the same, different) lengths of time.
2. Once a plant has started to grow and develop, the environment and the (weather, plant's life span, gardener) determine how long the plant lives.
3. Even if the environment is (cruel, indifferent, kind) to a plant, plants do not live forever.
4. Trees are usually (annuals, biennials, perennials).
5. The giant sequoias in California are some of the (newest, oldest, youngest) living perennials on earth.
6. Plants are divided into groups according to their (environment, life span, height).

Reproduction

Lesson 7

All plants do not reproduce in the same way. Reproduction in plants can take place in one of two basic ways: by asexual reproduction or by sexual reproduction.

The first method, asexual reproduction, is the simpler way for plants to reproduce. When a plant undergoes asexual reproduction, one of the plant's cells divides into two. Each cell produces another set of genes and then splits into two. In this way, the total number of cells in the plant is increased. When a strawberry plant makes runners, it is reproducing the runners asexually. Many plants, including the primitive plants referred to in an earlier lesson, only reproduce asexually.

The second method, sexual reproduction, requires a sperm and an egg. When the sperm and egg from plants merge or join one another, they form a single new cell. This single cell then divides into two cells. These two cells in turn divide into four cells. This dividing of the cells continues until a whole new plant is produced.

Along the way the cells in the new plant become specialized. Some cells become leaf cells, and others become stem or root cells. Advanced plants reproduce by sexual reproduction. You will learn more about pollination and the sexual reproduction of flowering plants in Unit 5.

Complete the following sentences. Write your answers on the lines provided.

1. Plants reproduce in one of two ways: by _____ or

   _____.

2. When a plant reproduces asexually, one of the plant's cells _____.

3. When a strawberry plant makes _____, it is reproducing asexually.

4. Sexual reproduction requires a _____ and an _____.

5. When the sperm and egg merge, they form a _____.

6. The single new cell divides into _____.

7. The dividing of the cells continues until a _____ is produced.

8. Along the way, some cells become _____.

9. Some cells become root or _____ or leaf cells.

10. Many primitive plants reproduce _____.

11. Advanced plants reproduce _____.

12. Asexual reproduction is _____ than sexual reproduction.

Review

R
E
V
I
E
W

Review your knowledge of plants and other living things. Write the answers to the following questions. Use complete sentences.

1. Why are plants given Latin names?

_____

_____

_____

2. What are some of the things that affect how long a plant lives?

_____

_____

_____

3. How is asexual reproduction different from sexual reproduction?

_____

_____

_____

4. How are plants different from other living things?

_____

_____

_____

5. What would our planet be like without plants?

_____

_____

_____

Nonvascular Organisms

Nonvascular organisms are some of the most primitive life forms. They rely on water coming to them since they have no **vascular tissue** to conduct water. Vascular tissue makes up a plant's **xylem** (which carries water and minerals) and **phloem** (which carries food).

Nonvascular organisms share other characteristics, too. They have no leaves, stems, or roots. Therefore, they are small and grow close to the ground. They often grow in mats or clusters and usually reach maturity quickly. Such growth is directly related to their appearance. Small organisms that have no roots, stems, or leaves to grow can become full-grown very fast.

Nonvascular organisms are not as specialized as vascular plants. They can grow in climates varying from cold, **arctic** regions to dry deserts. All they need is a rock, tree, or soil to grow on plus wind or rain to bring them **nutrients**.

This unit will discuss several kinds of simple nonvascular organisms: fungi, algae, lichens, and mosses. Of these, only mosses are considered to be plants.

A Complete the following sentences. Write your answers on the lines provided.

1. Nonvascular organisms are some of the most _____ life forms.

2. Nonvascular organisms are _____ and grow close to the ground.

3. They usually reach maturity _____.

4. A small organism that has no _____ to grow can become full-grown fast.

5. Nonvascular organisms are not as specialized as _____ plants.

B Write the answers to the following questions. Use complete sentences.

1. How do nonvascular organisms get water? _____

_____

2. What is vascular tissue? _____

_____

3. What are the characteristics of nonvascular organisms? _____

_____

4. How do nonvascular organisms grow? _____

_____

5. Where do nonvascular organisms grow? _____

_____

Fungi (singular: *fungus*) are primitive life forms. Once they were considered plants. But they do not have true roots, leaves, or stems. They do not contain chlorophyll in their cells. *Chlorophyll* is the chemical that makes plants look green. Many plants use chlorophyll to absorb light and to make food during photosynthesis. Fungi cannot make their own food. They absorb food from their surroundings.

Fungi can be divided into three groups: mushrooms, molds, and yeasts. Mushrooms are often easy to recognize. Some look like little umbrellas. Some mushrooms, such as oyster mushrooms and shitake mushrooms, are **edible.** However, many mushrooms are poisonous. Some fungi live and grow on other organisms. They are parasites. Others, such as the growths found on fallen trees, are **saprophytes.** Saprophytes live on dead matter. Fungi saprophytes break down the trees and make them into soil.

Another fungus, *Penicillium,* is a fuzzy mold that grows on citrus fruits, books, leather, lumber, and bread. The drug penicillin, which is made from this mold, has been widely used to fight many diseases. Other helpful molds are used to make cheeses. Bleu cheese, for example, is made by a mold. The cheese's sharp taste and blue color are caused by the mold growing in it.

Yeasts are another group of fungi. They grow as single cells. *Saccharomyces* is a yeast that ferments sugar to produce alcoholic drinks as well as alcohols used in industry. Yeast is also used in bread making. The yeast is added to a warm liquid sweetened with honey or sugar. The production of the gas carbon dioxide causes the bread to rise.

A Match the sentence parts by writing the letter on the line provided.

_____ 1. Plants use chlorophyll	a. yeasts.
_____ 2. Chlorophyll is also the chemical	b. and saprophytes.
_____ 3. Mushrooms often look	c. molds.
_____ 4. Fungi include parasites	d. to absorb light during photosynthesis.
_____ 5. One group of fungi is called	e. that makes plants look green.
_____ 6. Another group of fungi is called	f. is used in bread making.
_____ 7. Yeast	g. leaves, roots, or stems.
_____ 8. Fungi do not have true	h. like little umbrellas.
_____ 9. The sharp taste and blue color	i. edible.
_____ 10. Oyster mushrooms are	j. growths found on fallen trees.
_____ 11. Saprophytes are the fungal	k. of bleu cheese is caused by the mold that is growing in it.

B Write the answers to the following questions. Use complete sentences.

1. What are fungi? _____

_____

2. How are fungi different from plants? _____

_____

_____

3. What are mushrooms? _____

_____

4. What does *Penicillium* produce? _____

_____

5. What makes bread rise? _____

_____

Mushrooms are fungi that are often easy to recognize. Some mushrooms are edible, but others are poisonous.

Algae (singular: *alga*) are also examples of simple, primitive organisms. Algae come in all shapes, sizes, and colors. They can be unicellular, colonial, or multicellular. A unicellular alga is one that is made up of only one cell. Colonial algae are a group of unicellular algae that live close to one another in a cluster, or colony. Multicellular algae are whole algae made up of more than one cell.

Most algae live in fresh or marine water, but many types can live in other damp places. Therefore, algae can be found in wet soil. Some forms can also be found on damp bark, bricks, or roof shingles.

One example of a marine, or saltwater, alga is ulva. It is also known as sea lettuce. Ulva is a long, flat sheet of alga only two cells thick. Sea lettuce is edible, and it is considered a **delicacy** by people who live in Asian countries. Ulva is unusual among primitive organisms because it can reproduce either asexually or sexually.

A Underline the word or phrase that completes each sentence correctly.

1. Algae come in all (packages and weights, shapes and sizes, sounds and colors).

2. Multicellular algae are (partial, half, whole) algae made up of more than one cell.

3. Most algae live in (air or dirt, fresh or marine water, closets or cabinets).

4. An example of a marine, or (fresh water, river water, saltwater), alga is ulva.

5. Ulva is a long, flat sheet of alga only (two inches, two cells, two feet) thick.

B Read the following statements. If the statement is true, write *True* on the line provided. If the statement is not true, write *False.*

_____ 1. Algae are only unicellular.

_____ 2. All algae are found in fresh water.

_____ 3. Algae never live in soil.

_____ 4. Ulva is also called sea lettuce.

_____ 5. Ulva is poisonous to eat.

_____ 6. Although it is a primitive organism, ulva can reproduce sexually.

_____ 7. Algae come in many colors.

_____ 8. Another name for marine water is saltwater.

_____ 9. A colony is a whole algae that is made up of more than one cell.

_____ 10. Unicellular algae are made up of many cells.

Lichens

Lichen is the name given to two organisms, an alga and a fungus, that live and grow together. These two organisms form a **symbiotic** relationship, which means that they are helpful to each other and need each other to live. The alga gets water and minerals from the fungus. The fungus gets food from the alga, which is able to photosynthesize it.

Lichens are often found living on bare rocks where little else is able to grow. They appear in one of three forms: crustlike, shrublike, or leaflike.

Lichens are very valuable. They are a source of food for animals, such as reindeer, who live in the arctic regions. In fact, the arctic lichens are called reindeer moss. Many lichens are also used to make perfumes. Some are a good source of dyes because of their varied colors.

Lichens are able to grow on bare rock.

A Underline the word or phrase that completes each sentence correctly.

1. An alga and a fungus that live together are called a (lichen, vascular organism, primitive plant).

2. An alga is able to (catch, photosynthesize, store) food.

3. Lichens are a source of (food, cells, stems) for animals.

4. The lichens in the Arctic are called (reindeer, ice, snow) moss.

5. Some lichens are good sources of (fuel, dyes, paper).

B Write the answers to the following questions.

1. What are lichens? _____

_____

2. What is a symbiotic relationship? _____

_____

3. What does the alga get from the fungus? _____

4. What does the fungus get from the alga? _____

5. Where do lichens grow? _____

_____

Mosses

Mosses are small organisms that grow in moist areas, especially under shade trees. Because they are small and grow close together, they look like a carpet. They are unable to draw water from the soil they live on because they have no vascular tissue. Even so, because mosses share more characteristics with plants than they do with other organisms, they are considered to be plants.

Mosses reproduce sexually. Under a microscope, the female part and the male part on the same plant can be seen. The female part, called an **archegonium**, contains an egg. The male part, called an **antheridium**, contains hundreds of sperm. Sperm are released when the antheridium absorbs water and bursts. The sperm fall into the cup-shaped archegonium. The sperm and egg fuse and then go through several stages. Eventually, moss plants produce spores. **Spores** are small, seedlike reproductive cells that can be carried by the wind. The spores hatch, or germinate, to produce new moss plants.

There are many kinds of mosses. One type known to gardeners is sphagnum, or peat moss. When it is dry, this moss can be burned as a household fuel because it gives off a lot of heat. Peat moss is also good at absorbing water. It is often mixed with soil in gardens to help keep moisture around a plant's roots.

A Complete the following sentences. Write your answers on the lines provided.

1. Mosses are small plants that grow in _____, _____ areas.

2. Mosses reproduce _____.

3. The female part, called an _____, contains an egg.

4. The male part, called an _____, contains hundreds of sperm.

5. Spores are small, _____ reproductive cells carried by the _____.

6. The spores _____, or germinate, to produce new moss plants.

7. One type of moss that is known to gardeners is sphagnum, or _____.

B Write the answers to the following questions.

1. How valuable are nonvascular organisms? Prove your answer by giving four examples.

_____

_____

2. Where can the following organisms be found: fungi, lichens, algae, and mosses?

_____

_____

Parts of Vascular Plants

Vascular plants contain vascular tissue. Tissue is the name given to a group of cells that work to do a specific function. Vascular tissues (xylem and phloem) carry water, minerals, and food throughout the plant. Plants with vascular tissue do not have to live near water or in damp places. Vascular plants pull water and minerals from the soil through their roots. The xylem tissue carries water and minerals from the roots to the other parts of the plants.

Some nonvascular organisms contain chlorophyll. They produce food in every cell. All vascular plants, on the other hand, produce their food only in their leaves. The food, made in the leaves by photosynthesis, is carried to the other parts of the plant by the phloem tissue.

Nonvascular organisms are short or spread out along the surface that they live on. Staying small and flat helps them collect water and minerals. Because vascular tissue carries needed chemicals and food throughout a plant, vascular plants can grow tall and wide. For this reason, vascular plants are easy to recognize. Examples include ferns, trees, grass, and flowering plants.

This flowering plant has buds, a flower, leaves, roots, and a stem. Vascular tissue is shown by a dark line.

A Complete the following sentences. Write your answers on the lines provided.

1. _____ plants contain xylem and phloem.

2. _____ is a group of cells in a plant that work to do a specific function.

3. Vascular plants pull _____ and _____ from the soil through their roots.

4. All vascular plants produce their own food, but they do it only in their _____.

B Write the answers to the following questions.

1. What does xylem do? _____

_____

2. What does phloem do? _____

_____

3. Why can vascular plants have tall stems? _____

_____

Equisetum

***Equisetum*, or horsetails, are very unusual plants.**

Equisetum is the Latin name for horsetails. *Equi* means "horse," and *setum* means "tail." *Equisetum* are ancient vascular plants. They are known to have grown millions of years ago because they have been found in fossils. Therefore, the *Equisetum* we see today are sometimes called living fossils.

Equisetum have an interesting life cycle. They are soft-stemmed plants that grow about 1 meter (3 feet) high. Their stem, called a **rhizome,** stays alive underground as a perennial. The stems above ground, which are annuals, grow and die during a single season.

The leaves on *Equisetum* are unusual looking. They are tiny and grow in **whorls** at several places on a stem. *Equisetum* stems are hollow inside, but the stem is made up of plant tissue that contains sand. The sand makes the stems rigid and abrasive. In fact, they are so abrasive that they have been used for cleaning floors, pots, and pans.

Read the following statements. If the statement is true, write *True* on the line provided. If the statement is not true, write *False*.

_____ 1. *Equisetum* is the Latin name for horsetails.

_____ 2. *Equi* means "tail," and *setum* means "horse."

_____ 3. *Equisetum* are ancient nonvascular organisms.

_____ 4. *Equisetum* have been growing only for a few thousand years.

_____ 5. The *Equisetum* rhizome grows underground.

_____ 6. The above-ground stem of *Equisetum* is a perennial.

_____ 7. *Equisetum* are soft-stemmed plants that grow about 2 meters (6 feet) high.

_____ 8. *Equisetum* stems contain abrasive sand that can be used for cleaning floors.

Ferns

Ferns are common in many gardens that have shaded areas. These plants grow very well in shady, moist spots. Young, tender fern leaves, called *fronds*, are eaten as vegetables in many parts of the world.

Ferns have roots, stems, and leaves. The vascular tissues are seen as veins in the large fronds. As they start to develop, these fronds are coiled. As they grow, the fronds uncoil.

Ferns grow in both tropical and **temperate** areas. Ferns that existed millions of years before animals and humans lived on earth are still very important today. When those ancient plants died, some of the ferns were pressed between layers of dirt and rock. The fossilized ferns eventually became a type of rock. The rock they turned into is called *coal,* which is mined as a source of fuel today.

Christmas ferns grow well in moist, shady spots.

A Match the sentence parts by writing the letter on the line provided.

_____ 1. Ferns   **a.** tropical and temperate, or nontropical, areas.

_____ 2. The fronds   **b.** the fronds uncoil.

_____ 3. As they grow,   **c.** have roots, stems, and leaves.

_____ 4. Ferns grow in   **d.** are coiled when they start to develop.

B Write the answers to the following questions.

1. Where do ferns grow? _____

2. What are fern leaves called? _____

3. How are ferns used in some parts of the world? _____

4. Where can a fern's vascular tissue be seen? _____

5. In what climates do ferns grow? _____

6. What is coal? _____

Cacti and Succulents

Cacti (singular: *cactus*) and their relatives are able to take in large amounts of water. They store this water in their roots, stems, and leaves. Because the water makes the plants very soft and juicy, cacti and their cousins are called **succulents.** When the weather is dry, succulents use their own internal water supply to live. All cacti are succulents, but not all succulents are cacti. The aloe vera plant described in Unit 8 is an example of a noncactus succulent.

Cacti are easy to identify. They come in many sizes and shapes. Some cacti have leaves, but others are leafless. Some have sharp spines, which are modified leaves, and others do not. However, all cacti have areoles, or small woolly cushions on the cactus body. These round bumps look like they are filled with hair. Areoles are important because new spines and leaves grow from them. Cacti bodies do everything that leaves do on other plants. They capture sunlight, store water, and produce food.

Prickly pear cactus can grow in dry, sandy soil.

Succulents come in many interesting shapes. Some appear as stars. Living stones, which look like small pebbles, are succulents that grow in South Africa. The boojum tree lives in Baja California, Mexico. This succulent tree, which can grow 18 meters (60 feet) high, has a very strange appearance: it looks like an upside-down carrot. When it rains, the boojum tree sprouts leaves. In its new leaves, it starts making food for a few weeks. Then it loses its leaves and part of its stem. The stem that is left turns into a spine. In the tree's trunk is enough food and water to keep it alive during another long dry spell. Succulents can grow in dry areas where other plants cannot survive.

■ Read the following statements. If the statement is true, write *True* on the line provided. If the statement is not true, write *False.*

_____ 1. When the weather is dry, succulents use rainwater to live.

_____ 2. Cacti are easy to identify.

_____ 3. Areoles are important because new roots grow from them.

_____ 4. Cacti leaves capture sunlight, store water, and produce food.

_____ 5. All cacti are succulents, and all succulents are cacti.

_____ 6. Boojum trees are succulents that store water in their trunks.

Pitcher Plants

Pitcher plants are very unusual. Since they are vascular plants, they contain xylem and phloem. Like many other plants, they are able to photosynthesize to produce their own food. However, they can do something else that few other plants can do. Pitcher plants are **insectivorous**—they eat insects.

Pitcher plants attract insects with their brightly colored pitchers, which grow from the stems. On the lips of the pitchers is a sweet liquid. As an insect eats this liquid, it enters the pitcher to look for more. Then it slips, falls into the water at the bottom of the pitcher, and drowns. The remains of the insect are absorbed by the plant for its nutrients.

Pitcher plants are insectivorous: they eat insects.

Write the answers to the following questions. Use complete sentences.

1. How are pitcher plants like other vascular plants? _____

   _____

2. How are pitcher plants unusual? _____

   _____

3. What does *insectivorous* mean? _____

   _____

4. What part of the pitcher plant attracts insects? _____

   _____

5. What is on the lip of the pitcher? _____

   _____

6. What happens to the insect when it enters the pitcher? _____

   _____

   _____

7. What does the plant do with the dead insect?

   _____

   _____

U N I T 3

Club mosses, or ground pines, are simple vascular plants. They are related to the true mosses. However, unlike true mosses, club mosses have water-conducting tubes, xylem and phloem, in their stems. In addition, unlike trees and flowering plants, club mosses have xylem and phloem that alternate with each other in both the stems and the roots. This system is unique among plants.

Like true mosses, club mosses reproduce by spores, which are produced at the base of their leaves. Club mosses produce yellowish-colored spores. They were once used for coating pills and also for making fireworks. The spores burn in the explosion and give the fireworks a yellowish appearance.

When club moss spores leave the plants, they live in the soil seven years as they develop into new plants. Then it takes 10 years for these new plants to grow above the ground surface. Thus it takes almost 20 years for each single club moss to complete its cycle from a spore to a **mature** plant.

Club mosses (ground pines) are simple vascular plants.

A Underline the word or phrase that completes each sentence correctly.

1. Club mosses, or ground pines, are simple (vascular, nonvascular, short-lived) plants.

2. Their water-conducting tubes are (cellulose, xylem and phloem, wood).

3. Like true mosses, club mosses reproduce by (xylem, spores, seeds).

4. Club moss spores were used for coating (candy, pills) and making (fireworks, pencils).

5. Unlike (flowering plants, true mosses, trees), club mosses have water-conducting tubes.

6. The xylem and phloem in club mosses alternate with each other in both the stems and roots; this system is (unique, common, always present) in vascular plants.

B Review your knowledge of vascular plants. In complete sentences, write the answers to the following questions. Use your own paper.

1. How are ferns that lived millions of years ago important to us today?

2. What improvements do vascular plants have over nonvascular organisms?

Gymnosperms and Angiosperms

All plants with seeds are split into two groups by botanists: angiosperms and gymnosperms. Trees and bushes are in both groups.

Gymnosperms, which include pine trees and their relatives, have cones that hold the plant's female egg and seed. The egg and seed are exposed or naked in the cone. In fact, the word *gymnosperm* means "naked seed" in Greek.

The second major group of plants are angiosperms. This term, translated as "enclosed seed," means that the plant's seeds are produced and stored in a matured, or fully developed, ovary, a protective seed case. This mature ovary is called a *fruit*. Angiosperms are able to produce flowers as well as fruit. The angiosperm group is in turn split into two large subclasses: the **monocots** and the **dicots.** A **seed leaf** is the part of a plant's seed that becomes a leaf when the plant matures. Whether a plant has one or two seed leaves determines whether it is a monocot or a dicot.

The monocots have a single seed leaf. Monocot flowers and petals grow in groups of three. Their leaves have parallel veins. Examples of monocots are lilies, corn, and common grasses. The palm tree is also a monocot. Dicots have two seed leaves. Their flowers and petals grow in groups of four or five. Dicot leaves have a network of veins that branch out. Examples of dicot plants are roses and pansies. The dicot group includes almost all of the familiar trees, except for the gymnosperms. For example, an oak tree is a dicot.

The illustrations on pages 26–27 show various plants identified as either gymnosperms or angiosperms. Notice the examples of monocot and dicot seed leaves shown on page 27.

A Read the following statements. If the statement is true, write *True* on the line provided. If the statement is not true, write *False*.

_____ 1. *Angiosperm* means "naked seed."

_____ 2. The mature ovary of an angiosperm is its fruit.

_____ 3. A pine tree is an example of a monocot.

_____ 4. Dicot leaves have a network of veins that branch out.

_____ 5. Monocot flowers and petals grow in groups of four or five.

B Write the answers to the following questions.

1. What are the two groups of plants with seeds called? _____

2. What does the Greek term *gymnosperm* mean? _____

3. Into what two groups are angiosperms divided? _____

Gymnosperms

Longleaf Pine

Giant Sequoia

Engelmann Spruce

Blue Spruce

Angiosperms

Monocots: One seed leaf | **Dicots: Two seed leaves**

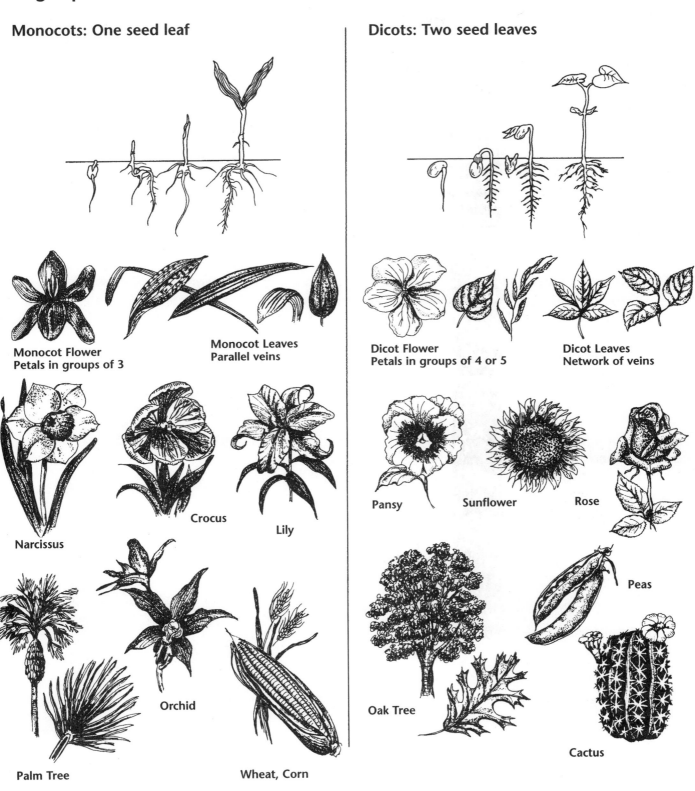

Monocot Flower
Petals in groups of 3

Monocot Leaves
Parallel veins

Narcissus

Crocus

Lily

Palm Tree

Orchid

Wheat, Corn

Dicot Flower
Petals in groups of 4 or 5

Dicot Leaves
Network of veins

Pansy

Sunflower

Rose

Peas

Oak Tree

Cactus

Trees have the same parts as other vascular plants: roots, stems or trunks, and leaves. Below the ground are the roots. They anchor the tree and also absorb water and minerals from the soil. Roots are of two types: taproots and fibrous. The dicots, the nonpine trees, all have taproots. A taproot is a large root with smaller roots branching from it. Fibrous roots are found on monocots. Fibrous roots are actually many roots together, all about the same size.

All trees have woody trunks made up of several layers. The outer bark helps protect the tree from disease, insects, and bad weather. The **cambium** layer goes all around the trunk like a ring and makes the tree trunk grow wider. Each year, the cambium grows a new layer of tissue, or **growth ring,** which is added to the inside of the trunk. When the cambium cells divide and grow outward, phloem is made. When they divide and grow toward the center of the tree, xylem is made.

The outer xylem layer is called *sapwood.* Sapwood is living tissue. It carries water and minerals. The inner xylem layer is called *heartwood.* Heartwood is able to carry water through its xylem when the tree is young. As the tree grows, these xylem tubes are pressed together. The heartwood dies and can no longer carry water. It becomes a darkened layer of dead cells. Heartwood gives strength to the tree.

Annual growth rings can be seen in a tree's sapwood and heartwood. Not only do the number of rings tell how old a tree is, but the sizes of the rings tell how much moisture fell during the years. A wide ring indicates a lot of rain or snow that year. A narrow ring indicates drier weather.

The trunk of a tree divides and forms many branches that spread out away from the trunk. On these branches are smaller stems, which have leaves. Just as in other plants, food is made in the leaves. The inner bark contains the phloem, which carries the food made in the leaves to the rest of the tree. Leaves come in a variety of shapes and sizes. Botanists classify leaves according to their shapes and edges.

 Write the answers to the following questions on your own paper.

1. What is in the center of a tree's trunk?
2. What is the heartwood's function when the tree is young?
3. What happens to the heartwood?
4. What does sapwood do?
5. Where are growth rings made?
6. What do growth rings indicate?
7. How are leaves classified?
8. What are taproots? Which plants have them?
9. What are fibrous roots? Which plants have them?

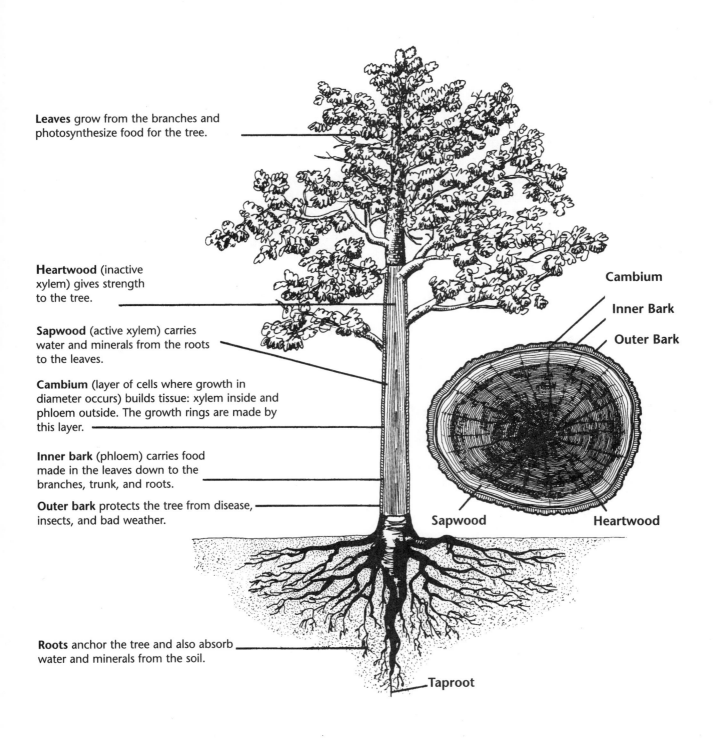

Leaves grow from the branches and photosynthesize food for the tree.

Heartwood (inactive xylem) gives strength to the tree.

Sapwood (active xylem) carries water and minerals from the roots to the leaves.

Cambium (layer of cells where growth in diameter occurs) builds tissue: xylem inside and phloem outside. The growth rings are made by this layer.

Inner bark (phloem) carries food made in the leaves down to the branches, trunk, and roots.

Outer bark protects the tree from disease, insects, and bad weather.

Roots anchor the tree and also absorb water and minerals from the soil.

Cambium

Inner Bark

Outer Bark

Sapwood

Heartwood

Taproot

Study the various parts of a tree shown in the illustration. The roots (in this case, a taproot) draw water and minerals from the ground. The trunk contains the outer bark, the cambium layer, the inner bark (phloem), the sapwood, and the heartwood. On the branches are the leaves, which photosynthesize food for the tree. The growth rings can be seen in the section of trunk shown on the right.

Longleaf Pines

Longleaf pines have long, thin needles. These needles are actually the plants' leaves, and they grow 30 to 46 centimeters (12 to 18 inches) long. The dark green, shiny needles grow in clusters of three. An illustration of the needles and cone of a longleaf pine can be seen on page 26.

Longleaf pines grow in the southeastern United States. These important pines produce gums, which are chemicals found in the trees' cells. When removed, gums are turned into turpentine or paint thinner.

Tapping a tree for gums and resins does not hurt the tree. However, longleaf pine resins can catch fire. During dry weather, longleaf pines burn easily, which can lead to widespread forest fires.

A Read the following statements. If the statement is true, write *True* on the line provided. If the statement is not true, write *False*.

_____ 1. Longleaf pines have short, flat needles.

_____ 2. The needles are the seeds of the longleaf pine.

_____ 3. Longleaf pines grow only in New York.

_____ 4. These trees are important because they produce gums.

_____ 5. Gums are used to make turpentine.

_____ 6. Tapping a longleaf pine for gums and resins hurts the tree.

B Write the answers to the following questions. Use complete sentences.

1. Is a longleaf pine a gymnosperm or an angiosperm?

_____

2. Where do longleaf pines grow?

_____

3. What are gums?

_____

4. What are gums used for?

_____

5. Why do longleaf pines burn easily?

_____

6. What do the needles of a longleaf pine look like?

_____

Eastern White Pines

Eastern white pines grow in the northeastern United States. They have been used as a source of **timber** for centuries.

White pines have cones and soft, blue-green needles. A white pine can be identified by counting its needles, five per cluster. Remember this hint: A five-needle pine is a white pine because the word *white* has five letters. White pines' cousins, the red pines, have three needles. How can someone remember that a three-needle pine is a red pine?

Newly planted white pines get diseases very easily. One disease is a fungus, pine blister rust. This disease is spread to white pines by **currants** and **gooseberries** growing nearby. If currants that have the fungus grow close to the white pine trees, the wind can carry the fungus to the tree.

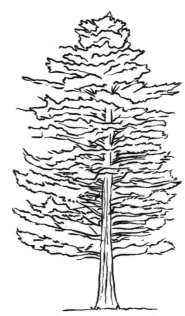

A white pine can be identified by counting its soft, blue-green needles, five per cluster.

Write the answers to the following questions. Use complete sentences.

1. Where do eastern white pines grow?

   _____

2. How are these trees used?

   _____

3. How can white pines be identified?

   _____

4. How can red pines be identified?

   _____

5. What disease affects white pines?

   _____

6. How is this disease spread to a white pine?

   _____

Douglas Firs

Douglas firs are not really **firs** but rather close relatives of **hemlocks.** Both firs and hemlocks are in the pine family. Douglas firs have flat, soft, short needles that grow around the twig.

Douglas fir cones are 5 to 8 centimeters (2 to 3 inches) long and have pointed tips, called *bracts,* that grow outward. These bracts grow between the cones' scales. Like other trees that have cones, Douglas firs are gymnosperms.

Douglas firs are the second largest trees in the United States. The only taller trees are the sequoias (giant sequoias and redwoods). Douglas firs are usually about 30 meters (100 feet) tall, but they can grow to 75 meters (250 feet). They can have a diameter of 2.4 meters (8 feet). Douglas firs are cut for timber and are often used to make plywood. They are the most common source of lumber in North America.

Douglas firs are the second tallest trees in the United States.

A Read the following statements. If the statement is true, write *True* on the line provided. If the statement is not true, write *False.*

_____ 1. Douglas firs are close relatives to hemlocks.

_____ 2. Both firs and hemlocks are in the pine family.

_____ 3. Douglas firs have long, round, hard needles.

_____ 4. Douglas fir needles grow around the twigs.

_____ 5. Douglas fir bracts grow between the cones' scales.

B Write the answers to the following questions. Use complete sentences.

1. What is one product made from Douglas firs?

_____

2. What are the tallest trees in the United States? the second tallest?

_____

Sugar Maples

Sugar maple trees are best known for their production of a sweet sap that is turned into sugar. You will learn more about the production of maple sugar in Unit 9. However, sugar maples are also good shade trees. They grow large and tall, as high as 30 meters (100 feet).

Sugar maple wood is very hard and is used to make furniture and cabinets. The branches of these trees are covered with leaves. In the fall, the leaves change color to yellow, orange, or deep red. Because they are such pretty trees, sugar maples are called **ornamental.**

The leaves of ornamental sugar maples turn beautiful colors in the fall.

Read the following statements. If the statement is true, write *True* on the line provided. If the statement is not true, write *False.*

_____ 1. Sugar maples can grow 30 meters (100 feet) tall.

_____ 2. The branches of sugar maples are covered with spines.

_____ 3. Sugar maples produce a sour-tasting sap.

_____ 4. Sugar maples are good shade trees.

_____ 5. The leaves of sugar maples turn blue, purple, and gray in the fall.

_____ 6. Sugar maples are called ornamental trees.

_____ 7. The wood of sugar maple trees is soft.

_____ 8. This wood is used to make furniture and cabinets.

_____ 9. Sugar maple trees can grow taller than Douglas firs.

_____ 10. Because they do not produce pine cones, sugar maples are gymnosperms.

White Oaks

White oaks grow in New England as well as all around the eastern half of the United States. Colonists were attracted to the beauty of this tree and often planted it. These trees are easy to identify because they have a light gray, scaly bark. Their leaves have seven to nine rounded **lobes,** or sections. These leaves are pinkish-red when they first open up in the spring. In the fall, they turn red again before they die.

White oaks, like all oak trees, produce acorns. This fruit is an important food for squirrels, chipmunks, and deer. Acorns were also eaten by Native Americans.

White oak trees grow slowly, but they can reach a height of 18 to 36 meters (60 to 120 feet). Oak wood is strong and lasts a long time. Today it is used as lumber for boats, furniture, and barrels.

■ Write the answers to the following questions. Use complete sentences.

1. Where do white oaks grow?

_____

2. What is the bark of a white oak like?

_____

3. What is the shape of white oak leaves?

_____

4. What color are white oak leaves when they first open in the spring?

_____

5. What color do these leaves turn before dying in the fall?

_____

6. What are acorns?

_____

7. Who or what uses acorns as food?

_____

8. How is the wood of white oaks used?

_____

9. How tall do white oaks grow?

_____

Giant Sequoias

Giant sequoias are cousins to the redwoods. Both types of trees were once very common and even grew as far north as the Arctic.

Giant sequoias have leaves like hemlock trees, members of the pine family. An illustration of the leaves and pine cone of the giant sequoia can be seen on page 26.

Giant sequoias and redwoods are some of the largest and oldest living things on earth. Many giant sequoias are thousands of years old. Their wood is brittle and coarse, but giant sequoias are a sight to see. These trees can reach heights of over 90 meters (300 feet) and also grow more than 30 meters (100 feet) around the trunk.

Today most sequoias are found in national parks where they are protected. No sequoias there are cut down to be used as lumber. These sequoia trees are the ancient giant heritage of our national parks.

A Read the following statements. If the statement is true, write *True* on the line provided. If the statement is not true, write *False*.

_____ 1. Giant sequoias are cousins to redwoods.

_____ 2. Both giant sequoias and redwoods have always been rare.

_____ 3. Giant sequoias have leaves like fir trees.

_____ 4. Giant sequoias are the youngest and smallest living things.

_____ 5. Giant sequoia wood is brittle and coarse.

_____ 6. Giant sequoias can grow to be 90 meters (300 feet) tall and 30 meters (100 feet) around the trunk.

_____ 7. Many giant sequoias are thousands of years old.

_____ 8. Giant sequoias are angiosperms.

_____ 9. Giant sequoias can grow taller than Douglas firs.

B Write the answers to the following questions. Use complete sentences.

1. Giant sequoia trees are not cut down for lumber. Why not?

_____

_____

2. Why are giant sequoia trees protected in our national parks?

_____

_____

Palm Trees

Palm trees grow in warm tropical regions of the world. Although they are trees, they are actually closely related to nontree monocot plants, such as lilies, bamboo plants, and grasses. The illustrations on page 27 show that a palm tree is classified with the monocot angiosperms. Notice how different the shape of the palm tree is from the shape of the dicot oak tree illustrated in the second column.

Although most palms grow in warmer tropical regions, the United States does have **native** palm trees. One is called the Washington palm. These trees grow in canyons and near waterholes in deserts. The fan-shaped leaves can be seen in the illustration on this page. These leaves grow from 1 to 2 meters (4 to 5 feet) wide. The Washington palm makes a flower that turns into a small, round, black fruit. Native Americans who lived in the deserts included this fruit in their diet.

Tropical palm trees are actually closely related to nontree monocot plants.

A Read the following statements. If the statement is true, write *True* on the line provided. If the statement is not true, write *False*.

_____ 1. Palm trees grow in cold arctic regions.

_____ 2. Palm trees are related to nontree plants.

_____ 3. The United States does not have a native palm tree.

_____ 4. The Washington palm grows near canyons and waterholes in the desert.

_____ 5. The leaves of the Washington palm are 4 to 5 meters (13 to 16 feet) wide.

_____ 6. The Washington palm produces a green fruit.

_____ 7. Some Native Americans ate this fruit as part of their diet.

B Answer the following questions. Use complete sentences and your own paper.

1. How do you know that palm trees are not gymnosperms?

2. Study the illustrations on page 27. How are monocot palm trees different from dicot oak trees? Consider the seed leaves, the shape of the trees, and the shape of the leaves.

Bonsai

Bonsai is an ancient Asian practice of keeping plants in pots. *Bonsai*, a Chinese word, means "tray-planted." People who have bonsai are keeping plants, usually trees, as **dwarfs**. These plants are carefully grown in the pots so that they look like a miniature part of nature.

Bonsai gardeners choose **woody plants** such as California junipers or Japanese black pines. These plants are grown in shallow containers. With an artistic eye, the gardener snips off branches to expose the trunk. Copper wire is wrapped around the branches to bend them gently. This bending gives the plant the same appearance as a tree that has been shaped by the weather for many years.

Over a period of many years, the bonsai plant is **pruned**, shaped, and reshaped. It must be watered frequently because the soil in a shallow container does not hold much moisture.

Small bonsai plants are carefully pruned to give them the appearance of old, weathered trees.

Bonsai gardening was developed into an art form by Chinese and Japanese aristocrats in the 1000s. It became a popular hobby in the U.S. in the early 1900s.

■ Read the following statements. If the statement is true, write *True* on the line provided. If the statement is not true, write *False*.

_____ 1. Bonsai is an ancient American practice of keeping plants in pots.

_____ 2. *Bonsai* is a French word for "tray-planted."

_____ 3. People who have bonsai are keeping plants as dwarfs.

_____ 4. Bonsai gardeners choose woody plants, such as California junipers or Japanese black pines.

_____ 5. Bonsai plants are grown in shallow containers.

_____ 6. Copper wire is used to shape the branches.

_____ 7. Bonsai plants do not need to be watered frequently.

_____ 8. Bonsai were first grown in China and Japan.

Review

Review your knowledge of trees. Write the answers to the following questions. Use complete sentences.

1. What is the major difference between angiosperms and gymnosperms?

_____

_____

2. What does the outer bark on a tree do?

_____

_____

3. What two things do the growth rings of trees tell foresters?

_____

_____

4. What kind of roots do dicots have? What kind of roots do monocots have?

_____

5. What are some of the oldest trees in the United States? Approximately how old are they?

_____

_____

6. Which two trees studied in this unit produce brightly colored leaves in the fall?

_____

_____

7. Which two trees studied in this unit produce fruit that is edible?

_____

8. What is the tallest tree studied in this unit? What is the smallest?

_____

9. Which of the following are gymnosperms and which are angiosperms: longleaf pine, white pine, Douglas fir, sugar maple, white oak, giant sequoia, and palm tree?

_____

_____

10. Which angiosperms from question 9 are dicots and which are monocots?

_____

_____

_____

Pollination in Flowering Plants Lesson 1

Producing flowers is the way many plants reproduce themselves. In the higher or more advanced vascular plants, the organs needed for sexual reproduction are in the flower. Study the illustration on this page. The anther and filament make up the stamen, which is the male part of the flower. The sepals and petals are sterile parts of the flower. Like leaves, they play no part in pollination.

Before a flower opens, it develops as a bud. The bud's opening its petals helps attract insects. Many flowers are shaped differently so that the insects pollinating the plant can get the pollen easily. These insects carry the pollen from the stamen of one plant to the pistil (female part) of another plant. The pistil is made up of the stigma, the style, and the ovary, which contains one or more ovules. The ovules turn into seeds.

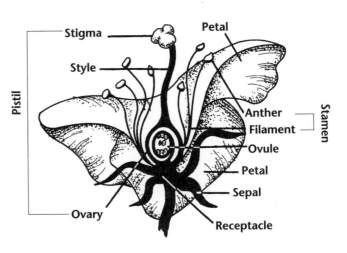

The parts needed for reproduction are contained in this plant's flower. Study these parts carefully.

Flowering plants are usually pollinated by insects. However, trees are usually pollinated by the wind. Some trees, like the turkey oak, have long stamens, called *catkins,* on their flowers. These stamens are long and flexible. When the wind blows, the catkins move and scatter ripened pollen. The pollen is carried from one tree to another.

At the top of the style is the stigma. The sticky stigma catches the pollen that is carried to it by insects or the wind. The pollen then sends out a long pollen tube that grows down the style. The sperm cell in the pollen fertilizes the egg cell in the ovule. This bringing together of sperm and egg cell produces an embryo—the beginning of a new plant. The embryo becomes a seed. When the plant dies or when the growing season ends, the seeds are scattered. They fall onto the ground where they germinate, or hatch, and grow into new plants. This process is a typical form of sexual reproduction in flowering plants.

A Underline the word or phrase that completes each sentence correctly.

1. Many plants reproduce themselves by producing (flowers, stems, roots).

2. The female sex organ in a plant is called the (stamen, pistil, sepal).

3. Before a flower opens, it develops as a (seed, pollen, bud).

4. Some flowers, like the turkey oak, have long (ovaries, stigmas, stamens) called *catkins.*

5. At the top of the style is the (soft, stiff, sticky) stigma.

B Write the answers to the following questions.

1. Why are flowers important to a plant? _____

_____

2. Why do flowers come in a variety of shapes and sizes? _____

3. What happens when insects are attracted to flowers? _____

4. What is the pistil? _____

5. How are trees usually pollinated? _____

6. What does the joining of one plant's sperm and another plant's egg produce? _____

_____

7. What does a plant embryo become? _____

8. What happens when seeds fall onto the ground and germinate? _____

_____

**Many insects and other animals and even the wind
help pollinate different plants. The illustration shows
a nectar-feeding bat visiting and pollinating agave.
These bats also pollinate the saguaro cactus.**

Wildflowers

Bright yellow flowers can be seen growing by highways. Clusters of white-petaled flowers on long green stems also wave along the roadsides. Some people call them weeds, but flowering weeds are actually wildflowers. Weeds and wildflowers grow fast, live for a short time, and are very hardy.

Wildflowers begin growing in the spring. Many can still be seen in the late fall, right up to the **killing frost.** Some wildflowers bloom for only a week, but many others will grow for an entire season, usually during the summer months.

Wildflowers add beauty to our countryside. They are found along roads and highways. They also grow in meadows, forests, hillsides, valleys, and wet areas such as **bogs.** Some wildflowers are fast disappearing because they are overpicked or because the areas where they grow are being developed. Many states now have laws that make it illegal to pick, move, or **transplant** wildflowers.

Colorful meadowfoam grows wild in western states.

A Read the following statements. If the statement is true, write *True* on the line provided. If the statement is not true, write *False*.

_____ 1. Wildflowers grow wild along roadsides.

_____ 2. Many wildflowers are called *weeds.*

_____ 3. Wildflowers start growing in the fall.

_____ 4. Wildflowers grow only in bogs.

_____ 5. Some wildflowers are disappearing.

_____ 6. Many states have passed laws to protect wildflowers.

B Match the sentence parts by writing the letter on the line provided.

_____ 1. Weeds and wildflowers grow   a. found along roads.

_____ 2. Wildflowers start   b. bloom for only one week.

_____ 3. Some wildflowers   c. growing in the spring.

_____ 4. Wildflowers are   d. fast, live for a short time, and are hardy.

Hibiscus

Hibiscus are native to the tropical parts of the world. Hibiscus are used as ornamental plants, as shrubs, and as **hedges.** The flowers of these plants are large and brightly colored. They all have a long stamen tube, which holds the stamens. Some hibiscus plants can grow from 4 to 5 meters (12 to 15 feet) high.

There are many varieties of hibiscus. The leaves of the hibiscus plants are shaped differently from one variety to the next. The yellow, red, and pink flowers are used by women in the tropics as adornments in their clothing and hair. In Hawaii, hibiscus blossoms are made into necklaces called *leis* (pronounced *lays*). These leis are often given as gifts to visitors in the Hawaiian islands.

Tropical hibiscus can be yellow, red, and pink.

Write the answers to the following questions. Use complete sentences.

1. Where are hibiscus native plants?

_____

_____

2. How are hibiscus plants used?

_____

_____

3. What is found in the stamen tube of these flowers?

_____

_____

4. What color flowers can hibiscus plants have?

_____

5. Where are hibiscus flowers made into leis?

_____

6. How are these leis used?

_____

_____

Marigolds

Marigolds are plants with yellow- to orange-colored flowers that are native to southern Europe. Today marigolds are found not only in Europe but all over the United States. They grow as annuals; however, in warm climates they will bloom year-round. When they die, they drop seeds that in turn produce new plants.

Marigolds are hardy ornamental plants. They are often grown in borders and in hanging baskets as well as planted in herb and rock gardens.

In addition, marigolds have historically been grown for their **culinary** properties. The dried and fresh petals of marigolds are edible. They are eaten in salads, cooked in stews, and also used to flavor cheese.

Hardy marigolds grow in both Europe and America.

A Read the following statements. If the statement is true, write *True* on the line provided. If the statement is not true, write *False*.

_____ **1.** Marigolds have red and purple flowers.

_____ **2.** Marigolds are native to Canada.

_____ **3.** Marigolds have been grown for their culinary properties.

_____ **4.** Marigolds are hardy plants.

_____ **5.** Marigold petals can be used to flavor cheese.

_____ **6.** When marigolds die, they drop seeds that in turn produce new plants.

_____ **7.** Marigolds are perennials; the plants grow for several seasons.

_____ **8.** Only the leaves of marigold plants are edible.

_____ **9.** Marigold plants were first grown in southern Europe and later brought to the United States.

_____ **10.** Marigolds will bloom year-round in cold climates.

B Write a definition for the following terms. Use a dictionary, if necessary.

1. culinary _____

2. ornamental _____

3. native _____

4. hardy _____

Water Lilies

Water lilies are dicots. They grow on top of water in warm to temperate regions of the world. Water lily flowers are open during the day. By late afternoon, however, their flowers are closed. These flowers come in a wide variety of colors: white, cream, pink, scarlet, blue, and purple.

Water lilies float on their large circular leaves. Their roots are buried in the bottom of the lake or pond. Under the lily pad, or leaf, are bubbles of oxygen. Although water lilies can cover a large part of a pond, they do not harm fish and other growing plants. Water lilies add oxygen to the water. Fish can breathe the oxygen.

Years ago, water lily seeds were used as a source of starch, oil, and protein. Parts of the lilies were roasted and eaten like potatoes. One type of water lily was used to make beer. Another type was grown for its **rootstocks**, which contained a dye. These rootstocks were used in Great Britain for dyeing wool a blue-black color.

Water lilies often cover a large part of a pond.

A Read the following statements. If the statement is true, write *True* on the line provided. If the statement is not true, write *False*.

_____ 1. Water lily flowers grow on the bottoms of ponds.

_____ 2. Water lilies take oxygen from the water.

_____ 3. Water lilies have flowers.

_____ 4. Water lily seeds were used as a source for starch, oil, and protein.

_____ 5. Some water lily rootstocks contain a dye.

_____ 6. Water lilies grow in temperate regions.

_____ 7. Water lily flowers are open at night.

_____ 8. Parts of water lilies are edible.

B Write the answers to the following questions. Use complete sentences.

1. How do water lilies float on top of the water? _____

_____

2. How are water lilies helpful to fish? _____

_____

Azaleas

Azaleas are flowering bushes. They are grown for their beautiful flowers, which can be orange, apricot, white, pink, or bright red in color. Azalea flowers are small. When a bush blooms, there are so many flowers that it is hard to see the rest of the bush.

Azaleas make beautiful additions to rock gardens and can also be used as shrub borders. Azaleas can be grown as houseplants, too.

Azaleas—like their cousins, the rhododendrons—are native to temperate regions in Asia and North America. Azaleas need a lot of moisture. Some azaleas grow at high **altitudes.** They thrive in partial shade with filtered sunlight.

Azaleas are grown for their beautiful, colorful flowers.

A Write the answers to the following questions.

1. To what other plants are azaleas related? _____

2. How are azaleas grown? _____

3. To what two parts of the world are azalea plants native? _____

4. Where do azalea plants thrive? _____

5. What color flowers do azaleas have? _____

B Write a complete sentence for each word or phrase. These sentences must be different from those given in the text.

1. Bush _____

   _____

2. Moisture _____

   _____

3. North America _____

   _____

4. Woodland _____

   _____

5. Azaleas _____

   _____

Daffodils

Daffodils are related to narcissus, a group of flowering bulbs. Bulbs are short, fleshy-leafed stems that grow underground. They are planted in the fall or spring. From the bulbs grow the stem, leaves, and flowers of the plants. Daffodils, which are also grown from bulbs, are one of the first flowers to appear in the spring.

Daffodils are ornamental. They are grown for their beauty both indoors and outdoors. They have six outer flowers and one single trumpet-shaped flower in the center. Daffodils are easy to grow because they will naturalize, or become established. Once planted, they will reproduce and grow perennially. Daffodils also do well as houseplants growing in pots indoors.

Ornamental daffodils can be grown indoors and outdoors.

A Rewrite the following sentences. Put each group of words in correct order so that the words express a complete idea.

1. that short are stems fleshy-leafed Bulbs underground grow

_____

2. outer Daffodils flower trumpet-shaped have and one center six flowers

_____

B Review your knowledge of flowering plants. Match the sentence parts by writing the letter on the line provided.

_____ 1. Wildflowers

_____ 2. Hibiscus

_____ 3. Marigolds

_____ 4. Water lilies

_____ 5. Azaleas

_____ 6. Daffodils

a. have edible yellow or orange petals.

b. are early spring flowers that grow from bulbs.

c. are disappearing because of increased land development.

d. are flowering bushes.

e. can be made into colorful leis.

f. were eaten as food and used to make beer and dyes.

C Write the *opposite* of each term.

1. native _____

2. pistil _____

3. tropical _____

4. hardy _____

Mid-Book Test

A Read the following statements. If the statement is true, write *True* on the line provided. If the statement is not true, write *False.*

_____ 1. The simplest form of any living thing is a cell.

_____ 2. Scientists who study plants are called *zoologists.*

_____ 3. Bacteria are used to make food such as cheese.

_____ 4. All bacteria are harmful and cause sickness.

_____ 5. Most angiosperms are made up of very few cells.

_____ 6. Photosynthesis is the process plants use to make food.

_____ 7. Latin names are used because they are easy to remember.

_____ 8. Fungi and algae are primitive organisms.

_____ 9. Yeasts are examples of fungi.

_____ 10. Annuals live for a year or less.

_____ 11. Trees are perennials.

_____ 12. All plants reproduce in the same way.

_____ 13. Asexual reproduction involves an egg and a sperm.

_____ 14. Lichens and mosses are nonvascular organisms.

_____ 15. Chlorophyll in a plant makes it look green.

_____ 16. A lichen is really an alga and a fungus growing together.

_____ 17. All succulents are cacti.

_____ 18. A pitcher plant eats insects.

_____ 19. A pine tree is an angiosperm.

_____ 20. The wood of the sugar maple is used for sugar.

_____ 21. Giant sequoias are some of the oldest living things on earth.

_____ 22. Bonsai are very large trees.

_____ 23. Flowering plants are usually pollinated by wind.

_____ 24. Hibiscus are sometimes used as hedges.

_____ 25. Marigold petals can be eaten.

B Complete the following sentences. Use the words in the box.

monocots	microscope	seed	penicillin
asexual	pollen	roots	phloem

1. A _____ must be used to look at plant cells.

2. _____ have petals in groups of three.

3. The drug _____ is made from mold.

4. The stigma in plants catches _____.

5. Food is carried to other parts of vascular plants by the _____.

6. The embryo of a plant eventually becomes a _____.

7. In _____ reproduction, a plant cell divides into two.

8. A tree absorbs water and minerals from the soil through its _____.

C Read the name of each organism. Write the word from the box that can be used to describe the organism.

gymnosperm	fungus	angiosperm	lichen	moss

1. mushroom   _____

2. Douglas fir   _____

3. mold   _____

4. daffodil   _____

5. reindeer moss   _____

6. peat   _____

7. cactus   _____

8. giant sequoia   _____

Types of Fruits

As an ovule turns into a seed, the ovary part of the pistil may grow large in size. This large ovary is a fruit, or a ripened ovary with one or more seeds. It takes a large amount of food and energy for plants to grow fruit. While plants make their fruits, the plants themselves stop growing. Once the fruits are mature, the other parts of the plants can start to grow again.

Fruits can be divided into four different types according to how the fruits develop from the plant's ovaries. A simple fruit is one that develops from one ovary; for example, pea pods. A fruit that grows from a group of ovaries in a single flower, such as a blackberry, is an aggregate fruit. A multiple fruit, such as a pineapple, is one that grows from ovaries in a group of flowers on the same branch. An accessory fruit is a fruit that grows from one or more ovaries along with the sepals or the receptacle (the part that supports the ovary) or both. An example would be a pear. Illustrations of the four types of fruits can be seen on this page.

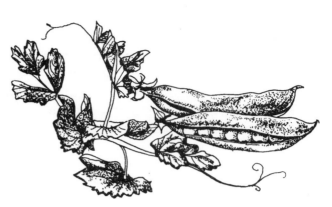

Pea pods are examples of simple fruits.

A blackberry is an example of an aggregate fruit.

A pineapple is an example of a multiple fruit.

A pear is an example of an accessory fruit.

Fruits can also be classified according to their appearance. A berry is a fruit that is soft and fleshy on the outside when the fruit is full grown. Grapes and tomatoes are berries. A drupe has a thin skin, a fleshy inside, and a hard pit in the center. Cherries, plums, and peaches are drupes. A legume is a fruit with a leathery outside. It splits along two seams. Beans, peas, and clover are legumes. A grain is a dry, one-seeded fruit with a seed coat and an ovary wall that have joined together. Corn, wheat, and oats are grains. It is easy to tell whether fruits are berries, drupes, legumes, or grains.

Pinching off some flower buds will help the plant make the other flowers bigger. Bigger flowers make bigger fruits. Perennial plants need to be pruned every year, or they will produce large fruit only every couple of years. Fruit tree growers prune their trees in order to grow large fruit every year.

The plant's seeds are protected in fruits. Seeds from a fruit may end up being scattered in a new area. Scattering helps guarantee that the seeds land in good places to grow into new plants.

Choose the correct answer to complete each of the following sentences. Write your answers on the lines provided.

1. A large, ripened _____ is a fruit.   (stamen, pistil, seed, ovary)

2. _____ are examples of accessory fruits.
   (Pea pods, Blackberries, Pineapples, Pears)

3. It takes a large amount of _____ for a plant to grow a fruit.
   (food and energy, minerals and vitamins, sunlight and water, air and water)

4. Fruits can be divided into _____ different types. (one, two, three, four)

5. According to their appearance, grapes and tomatoes are _____.
   (drupes, grasses, berries, legumes)

6. A _____ is a fruit with a leathery outside.
   (tomato, berry, legume, peach)

7. Pinching off some flower buds helps plants make other _____ bigger.
   (fruits, seeds, flowers, berries)

8. Bigger flowers make bigger _____. (leaves, fruits, stems, roots)

9. The _____ are protected in fruits.   (seeds, ovules, pistils, stamens)

10. _____ helps guarantee that perennial plants grow large fruit every year.
    (Scattering, Pruning, Growing, Pinching)

How Seeds Are Scattered
Lesson 2

Seeds need to be scattered so that new plants will grow. If all of the seeds stayed close to the parent plants, too many plants would grow in the same area. All of these plants would compete for sunlight, water, minerals, and space. When seeds are scattered, there is less overcrowding. Each plant can then obtain enough light, water, and minerals to grow properly.

Seeds are scattered in several ways. The wind helps scatter seeds. Some seeds are lightweight. The wind can blow them great distances. The seeds of some plants, such as maple trees, have wings. Other kinds of seeds have hairy exteriors. Wind can carry these seeds a long way.

Animal can scatter seeds. Some fruits have hooks that get caught in the fur of wild animals. When an animal brushes against the plant, the fruit and its seeds fall off. Many fruits are eaten by animals. A bird may eat a grape, fly away, and leave the grape's seeds far from the parent grape plant.

Seeds can float and be carried great distances by water. **Tumbleweeds** scatter their seeds as they roll across the land. Some plants have fruits that explode and toss the seeds far away from the parent plants. Out of the many scattered seeds, some will find the right environment to grow into new plants.

A Rewrite each group of words so that the words express a complete idea.

1. seeds scatter Wind helps

_____

2. great distance a not are heavy, can and the wind Seeds carry them

_____

3. seeds have wings hairy or exteriors plants Some have that

_____

4. can way carry long these seeds a Wind

_____

B Write the answers to the following questions.

1. Why do seeds need to be scattered? _____

2. What happens when plants are not spread out? _____

3. What are three ways in which seeds are scattered? _____

4. What holds some seeds in animals' fur? _____

5. How do tumbleweeds scatter their seeds? _____

Apples

People have grown apples since ancient times. Apples were cut up and stored as dried fruits to be eaten during the winter months. In the 1600s, apple trees were brought to North America from England. Today apple trees are found all over the United States.

Apples are **nutritious.** They contain carbohydrates and vitamins A and C. Many minerals, such as calcium and iron, are found in apples. A ripe apple is also about 85 percent water.

Apples are grown in thousands of varieties. They are grouped according to their color, size, and flavor. Each type of apple, depending on its purpose, is called a fresh-eating, cooking, cider, or a drying apple. Each variety of apple has a name. For eating, the Golden Delicious and McIntosh are favorites. Jonathan and Granny Smith are good cooking apples.

There are thousands of varieties of apples. This photograph shows a McIntosh.

A Read the following statements. If the statement is true, write *True* on the line provided. If the statement is not true, write *False*.

_____ 1. Because apples rot easily, they cannot be dried.

_____ 2. Apples have been grown and eaten for only a short time.

_____ 3. Apples were brought to North America from England.

_____ 4. Apples are grouped according to their size, color, and flavor.

_____ 5. Apples are also grouped according to whether they are good for eating, cooking, making cider, or drying.

_____ 6. Apples are not nutritious.

_____ 7. Apples contain calcium and iron.

_____ 8. Apples are 85 percent water.

B Write the answers to the following questions.

1. What two types of apples are good for eating? _____

_____

2. What two types of apples are good for cooking? _____

_____

Watermelons

Watermelons probably first grew in northern Africa. Now they are a favorite garden fruit and are grown all over the United States.

Watermelons are annuals. They grow long vines that spread out 2 to 3 meters (6 to 10 feet) long. Each plant produces three or four watermelons. Each watermelon can weigh as little as 1 kilogram (2 pounds) or as much as 18 kilograms (40 pounds). It can be perfectly round or long and stretched out in shape. About 95 percent of the watermelon is water. The fruit contains large seeds and very red pulp. The pulp, the part that is eaten, has vitamins and is sweet tasting. Many people think that a watermelon is the perfect food to eat on a hot summer day.

Watermelons are a favorite garden fruit in the United States.

A Underline the word or phrase that completes each sentence correctly.

1. Watermelons probably first grew in (South America, the United States, northern Africa).

2. Watermelons are a favorite garden (fruit, berry, vegetable).

3. Each watermelon plant produces (one or two, three or four, 10 or 12) watermelons.

4. About (1 percent, 50 percent, 95 percent) of a watermelon is water.

5. Watermelons contain large seeds and very red (fruit, pulp, skin).

6. The pulp contains (fat, vitamins, protein).

7. The (bitter, sour, sweet) pulp is the part of a watermelon that is eaten.

B Write the answers to the following questions. Use complete sentences.

1. How long are watermelon vines? _____

_____

2. How would you describe a watermelon?_____

_____

3. Why are watermelons so juicy to eat? _____

_____

4. Why would a watermelon taste good on a hot summer day?_____

_____

Oranges

Oranges are perennial fruits that grow on trees. They first grew in India and China. Today they are grown in warm climates all over the world. In the United States, they are grown in Florida, California, Texas, and Arizona.

Oranges may or may not contain seeds. Those without seeds are called *navel oranges*. The skin covering an orange is called the *rind*. It protects the fruit and seeds while they mature. This bitter-tasting rind is removed before the fruit inside is eaten. Oranges are very nutritious. They are good sources of vitamin C, vitamin A, and sugar. Oranges are not fattening, and people on diets love to eat them. Oranges are usually eaten fresh. However, the juice of an orange makes a refreshing and popular drink.

Notice the blossoms near the ripe orange.

A Match the sentence parts by writing the letter on the line provided.

_____ 1. Oranges are perennial

_____ 2. Oranges were first grown

_____ 3. In the United States,

_____ 4. The juice

_____ 5. Oranges contain

a. vitamin C.

b. oranges are grown in Florida, California, Texas, and Arizona.

c. fruits that grow on trees.

d. in India and China.

e. of an orange makes a refreshing drink.

B Read the following statements. If the statement is true, write *True* on the line provided. If the statement is not true, write *False*.

_____ 1. Oranges are grown all over the world.

_____ 2. Oranges are not nutritious.

_____ 3. Oranges contain sugar.

_____ 4. Oranges are fattening.

_____ 5. Orange rinds are sweet tasting.

_____ 6. Oranges always have seeds.

_____ 7. The rind of an orange protects the fruit and seeds.

_____ 8. Oranges grow in cold climates.

_____ 9. Navel oranges do not have seeds.

_____ 10. Oranges are never eaten fresh.

Nuts

Nuts are fruits with a hard outer shell. Many nuts, such as walnuts and pecans, are edible. Like other fruits, nuts are grown **commercially** in orchards. They usually grow on deciduous trees. The leaves of these trees (unlike evergreens) fall off at the end of the growing season. Nuts also grow in all kinds of climates.

The cashew is a favorite nut to eat, but the cashew tree is a member of the poison ivy family. Cashews are safe to eat only after they have been roasted. Roasting destroys any toxin that may be in the raw nut.

Pecans are really hard seeds from tall, spreading trees that can grow over 30 meters (100 feet) high. Pecans are grown in the Mississippi River valley as far north as Indiana and Illinois. These nuts grow in clusters of four to twelve and are from 4 to 6 centimeters ($1\frac{1}{2}$ to $2\frac{1}{2}$ inches) long. There are many varieties of this native plant. Pecans are one of the most important nut crops grown in the United States today.

Fifteen types of trees grow walnuts. Some of these trees originated in the **Mediterranean countries** of southern Europe and in Asia. Some kinds are native to North and South America. All the varieties of these trees grow delicious and edible nuts, but only one variety of the trees in the United States is grown commercially. Walnuts are grown both for eating and for their oil. The kernels contain a great amount of oil, which is used for cooking and making paints. Like cashews and pecans, walnuts are very popular in the United States.

A For each word, write a word that means the *opposite*.

1. edible_____   3. hard _____

2. deciduous _____   4. raw _____

B Identify the nut described in each sentence. Write your answers on the lines provided.

_____   1. These nuts grow in clusters of four to twelve.

_____   2. These nuts are safe to eat only after they have been roasted.

_____   3. These nuts are grown for eating and for their oil.

_____   4. The tree that grows these nuts is a member of the poison ivy family.

_____   5. These are one of the most important nut crops in the United States.

_____   6. These nuts grow on 15 varieties of trees, but only one type of tree is grown commercially in the United States.

_____   7. These nuts grow in the Mississippi River valley.

Bananas

Banana plants and their fruits have been known since ancient times. Botanists believe that they were first grown in Asia. Today they are grown wherever consistently warm climates are found.

Thousands of years ago, the banana was a fruit without any flavor. It had many bitter black seeds. Then people started to **cultivate** and improve the banana. Today bananas are known for their delicious, sweet taste.

Bananas contain vitamin A, which makes them easy to **digest**. They are also rich in vitamins B and C, include important minerals such as potassium, and contain a high amount of sugar. Bananas can be eaten raw, cooked, or baked.

A Write the answers to the following questions.

Bananas need a warm climate to grow well.

1. What was the banana like thousands of years ago? _____

2. What are three ways in which bananas may be eaten? _____

B Write a definition for each word. Use a dictionary, if necessary.

1. ancient _____

2. climate _____

3. flavor _____

4. digest _____

C Review your knowledge of fruits. Match the sentence parts by writing the letter on the line provided.

_____ 1. Apples   **a.** are high in vitamin C. All varieties have rinds; some have seeds.

_____ 2. Watermelons   **b.** can be eaten fresh, cooked, or dried and made into cider.

_____ 3. Oranges   **c.** are fruits with hard outer shells.

_____ 4. Nuts   **d.** have been improved; they now taste sweet.

_____ 5. Bananas   **e.** contain large seeds and sweet, red pulp.

Cereals, Grasses, and Vegetables

Grasses, cereals, and vegetables are all plants that are grown for agricultural purposes.

Grasses are monocots. They produce flowers and have one seed leaf. They have leaves with parallel veins, which means that the veins all run in one direction. Veins are part of the vascular part of the plant leaf. Grasses have their vascular sections in their stems. The center of their stems is called the **pith.** The round, hollow stems have solid **nodes,** or **joints.** Grasses grow a portion of their stems underground.

Grasses grow underground, produce fibrous roots, and then make new plants. This process explains how grasses spread so quickly. Grass inflorescenses, or flower clusters, are small, scaly units called *spikelets.* Grasses can be identified by their inflorescenses.

Wheat, corn, and tomatoes are examples of agricultural crops.

Cereals are grasses that are grown for their edible seeds, or grains. The most commonly grown cereals worldwide are wheat, rice, corn, barley, oats, rye, sorghum, and millet. Wheat, corn, and rice support most of the world's population. Cereal crops are classified as annuals.

Vegetables are commonly thought of as the parts of plants eaten during a meal. In contrast, fruits are often considered as desserts. The word *vegetable* is misleading because many foods that are called vegetables are really fruits. For example, tomatoes are usually eaten during a meal in a sauce or a sandwich, but botanists know that tomatoes are fruits, the ripened ovaries of a seed plant.

 Underline the word or phrase that completes each sentence correctly.

1. (Dicot, Grain, Monocot) grasses produce flowers and one seed leaf.

2. Grasses have their vascular sections in their (roots, stems, leaves).

3. In the center of a grass stem is the (pith, xylem, cambium).

4. The root systems of grasses are always (long, fibrous, short).

5. Grasses grow a portion of their (flowers, leaves, stems) underground.

6. Two cereals that are important to the world's population are (barley and rye, oats and sorghum, wheat and corn).

7. Botanists know that tomatoes are (fruits, vegetables, cereals).

8. Cereals are grasses grown for their (stems, seeds, roots).

Oats

Oats are grown in temperate areas on most continents of the world. They were grown in Europe for centuries and were one of the first crops brought to the Americas.

The fruit of the oat plant is the edible part. This edible, dry fruit is called a *caryopsis.* A caryopsis is a fruit with a single seed and an attached hull or pericarp. The pericarp develops from the ovary wall. The seed and hull are so close together that a single body, called a *grain,* is formed.

Of all the cereal grains, oat seeds contain the greatest amount and the best quality of protein. Nutritious oats are used to make oatmeal and other hot and cold breakfast cereals. Oat plants are also grown as feed for livestock.

High protein makes oats a nutritious cereal grain.

 Write the answers to the following questions. Use complete sentences.

1. What is the edible part of an oat plant?

_____

2. What is the fruit of an oat plant called?

_____

3. How is a grain formed?

_____

4. What are oats used for?

_____

5. Why are oats nutritious?

_____

6. Where do oat plants grow?

_____

7. Where did oats in the Americas come from?

_____

8. What is a pericarp?

_____

Wheat

Wheat may have been the very first crop that was **domesticated** and cultivated by humans. Historians know that people living about 11,000 years ago grew wheat.

Annual varieties of wheat were preferred by early people. Wheat was grown in areas next to rivers that flooded every year. This flooding made the area fertile. The annual plants were grown and harvested before new floods came and washed the plants away.

Wheat is grown for use in bread making. Two types are planted, spring wheat and winter wheat. Spring wheat is planted in the spring and grown during the summer. It is harvested in the fall. Winter wheat is planted in the fall and becomes a seedling by winter. Then it lies **dormant** through the winter months. In some semiarid western areas of the United States, melting snowfall helps provide moisture for winter wheat to begin growing again during the warmer spring months. Winter wheat is harvested in the early summer. In many areas, wheat is the most important crop.

People have grown wheat for thousands of years.

Complete the following sentences. Write your answers on the lines provided.

1. Wheat may have been the first crop that was _____ and cultivated by humans.

2. Historians know that people living about _____ years ago grew wheat.

3. _____ varieties of wheat were preferred by early people.

4. Wheat was grown next to rivers that _____ every year.

5. Wheat is grown for use in _____.

6. _____ types of wheat are grown.

7. _____ wheat is planted in the spring and harvested in the fall.

8. _____ wheat is planted in the fall and harvested in early summer.

9. Winter wheat lies _____ during the winter months.

10. Melting snow provides _____ for winter wheat, which helps it begin growing in the spring.

Corn is often called "king," the monarch of grain crops in North America as well as the most grown vegetable. Corn is well liked by farmers for several reasons.

It adapts easily. It can grow in semiarid or very dry regions. It can grow in cold regions and at low or high altitudes. Corn can be grown just about anywhere—on flat land, in woods, and on hillsides. Corn plants do not need to be planted in **tilled** soil to grow well.

Corn also photosynthesizes very efficiently. The leaves are broad enough to be exposed to plenty of sunlight while not shading the rest of the plant too much to prevent growth.

The ears contain the corn kernels, or grains. The husk prevents rain and birds from damaging the grains. Each ear of corn has about 18 rows of kernels. Many new plants can grow from the seeds of a single corn plant. Corn, along with wheat, supports most of the world's population.

Corn is a major grain crop.

Write the definition for each word. Use a dictionary, if necessary.

1. monarch_____

2. photosynthesize _____

3. adapt _____

4. husks_____

5. kernels _____

6. semiarid _____

7. tilled _____

8. population_____

9. altitude_____

10. support_____

Wild Rice

Another name for wild rice is wild oats. These plants are really members of the oat, not the rice, family. However, wild oats look so much like real rice that they are sometimes called *wild rice.* Wild rice is native to North America. In fact, it and corn are the only native grains that this continent has produced. Wild rice was a food source for Native Americans, explorers, trappers, and traders for centuries.

Wild rice grows in **swamplands** and along the shores of rivers and lakes. The plants grow from 1 to 2 meters (4 to 8 feet) tall. Some wild rice is harvested by Native Americans in the same way their ancestors harvested it centuries ago. The people ride in a canoe or boat between the rice plants, pull a handful of the plants over the side of the boat, and smack them. The mature rice falls into the boat.

Wild rice is a nutritious grain that has not been commercially grown extensively. Because of limited quantities, wild rice is expensive.

A Match the sentence parts by writing the letter on the line provided.

_____ 1. Another name for wild rice

_____ 2. Wild oats look so

_____ 3. Wild rice is native

_____ 4. Wild rice is a

_____ 5. Wild rice is expensive

a. much like real rice that they are called *wild rice.*

b. to North America.

c. nutritious grain.

d. because it is not grown in large quantities.

e. is wild oats because wild rice is not really a member of the rice family.

B Read the statements. If the statement is true, write *True* on the line provided. If the statement is not true, write *False.*

_____ 1. Wild rice is related to corn.

_____ 2. Wild rice is really wild oats.

_____ 3. Wild rice is native to Asia.

_____ 4. Wild rice looks like real rice.

_____ 5. Wild rice is grown in deserts.

_____ 6. Some wild rice is harvested by Native Americans.

_____ 7. Wild rice was a food source for Native Americans, trappers, explorers, and traders.

C On your own paper, write the definition for each word. Use a dictionary, if necessary.

1. commercial   2. nutritious   3. canoe

Kenaf

Kenaf, also called Indian **hemp,** is considered one of the most promising new crops in the United States. Kenaf is a relative of cotton and **okra.** Its stalk grows over 4 meters (12 feet) tall and matures fairly quickly. When stripped of its flowers and leaves, a stalk of kenaf looks like a stalk of bamboo.

Kenaf is being commercially grown in Southern states from Virginia to California. It is harvested, dried in the field, and taken to newsprint mills. At the mills, kenaf's outer bark and inner core fibers are processed into newsprint. Newsprint made from kenaf is brighter and stronger; it prints better than newsprint made from most wood pulp. Kenaf costs less to make into newsprint, too. Fewer chemicals and less energy are needed to process it. Agricultural experts predict that kenaf will be grown on more than a million acres in less than a few decades. Kenaf has a future as a big cash crop.

Kenaf, a new source of pulp, grows over 4 meters (12 feet) tall. Outer kenaf fibers are peeled back. Inside is a light-colored inner core of short, woody fibers.

■ Write the answers to the following questions.

1. To what plants is kenaf related? _____

_____

2. What is another name for kenaf? _____

_____

3. Where is kenaf being grown commercially? _____

_____

4. What is kenaf used for? _____

_____

5. Why is kenaf better than wood pulp? _____

_____

Tomatoes

Tomato plants are native to South America. The Spanish and Portuguese brought tomatoes to Europe in the mid-1500s, where they were first eaten as a vegetable. However, tomatoes are actually the fruit of the tomato plant. Remember that a fruit is a ripened ovary of a seed plant.

Wild varieties of tomatoes still grow in Peru and Texas. Today, however, many tomatoes are grown all over the world as **hothouse plants**. Cultivated tomatoes look very different from their wild cousins. They can have red, orange, or yellow skins when ripe, and they can be big or small, round or pear-shaped. Even a round-bottomed, square-sided variety is grown; these tomatoes are perfectly shaped for fitting into cans.

Tomatoes are very popular and nutritious. Tomato paste, ketchup, and juice are widely consumed in America. Tomatoes are eaten raw, added to salads, and cooked into sauce. The fruits contain vitamin C, some vitamin A, and very few calories. Tomatoes are grown on farms and in garden plots.

These Maryland tomatoes are ripe for picking.

 Underline the word or phrase that completes each sentence correctly.

1. Tomato plants are native to (Asia, North America, South America).

2. (Mexicans and Native Americans, Spanish and Portuguese, Italians and Germans) brought tomatoes to Europe, where they were eaten as vegetables.

3. Tomatoes are actually the (fruit, stem, root) of the tomato plant.

4. Tomatoes are grown all over the world as (hothouse, wild, domesticated) plants.

5. Wild varieties of tomatoes still grow in (Brazil and Mexico, Peru and Texas, California and Canada).

6. Cultivated tomatoes have a different appearance than that of their (wild, hothouse, planted) cousins.

7. Cultivated tomatoes can have red, orange, or yellow (leaves, skins, flowers) when ripe.

8. Tomatoes contain vitamins (C and A, C and B, A and D).

Vegetables in the Wild

Today when people want to eat vegetables, they usually go to a supermarket and buy them from the produce section. However, long before vegetables were stored, canned, or frozen, they grew in the wild. For centuries, people would forage for vegetables in the fields and woods close to where they lived.

Native Americans ate a variety of vegetables. Some Native Americans raised vegetables, such as corn or squash, in gardens. Many picked vegetables growing in the wild. Onions, dandelion greens, **Jerusalem artichoke tubers**, and acorn meats were a few of the plants they collected and used as vegetables. Native Americans ate the wild vegetables fresh or preserved them for later use. Wild plants provided an important source of food.

Native Americans showed European settlers what plants to look for, which were edible, and which were poisonous. They showed the colonists how to prepare and preserve the vegetables. Salting, drying, and pickling vegetables were the most common methods of preserving food. Such methods enabled people to have vegetables to eat during the winter months.

Many of the vegetables eaten hundreds of years ago are still grown and eaten today. Maize, or corn, is one such vegetable. In fact, corn is the most commonly grown vegetable in the world today.

Write the answers to the following questions. Use complete sentences.

1. Where did people long ago get vegetables?_____

_____

2. How were vegetables preserved? _____

_____

3. What vegetables did some Native Americans grow in gardens?_____

_____

4. What wild plants did many Native Americans collect and use as vegetables? _____

_____

5. How did Native Americans help European settlers?_____

_____

6. Where do most people get vegetables today? _____

_____

7. What is the most commonly grown vegetable today? _____

_____

Types of Vegetable Gardens

Vegetable gardens are a favorite of those who enjoy eating freshly picked foods. Even in a small area, several different types of vegetables can be raised. The vegetables can be eaten fresh or preserved. When preserved, vegetables can be eaten during the winter months when fresh vegetables are out of season. For many people, having fresh vegetables to eat makes growing them worthwhile.

There are several types of gardens. In some gardens, many different vegetables are grown in separate rows. Such large gardens are only for people with enough land. People who live in the country might plant this type of garden.

For city people, potted vegetable gardens are more practical. Many vegetables grow well in pots. If a city dweller has a terrace or balcony, a single large pot can hold several plants. With only a few pots, a person can have quite a large garden. The potted plants also make a terrace or balcony more attractive.

For people with a small plot of land, raised **bed** gardens work well. Boards or railroad ties are used to form square beds. Topsoil is added to raise the bed about 10 centimeters (4 inches) higher than the ground outside of it. Every bit of the bed is covered with vegetable plants. Because the bed is small, picking the vegetables is easy. Raising the bed helps drain the soil around the vegetable plants' roots. If a plant sits too long in water, the roots can rot and the plant dies. Raised bed gardens use space efficiently and can yield many fresh vegetables.

A Write the answers to the following questions. Use complete sentences.

1. Why do people plant vegetable gardens? _____

_____

2. Why might people who live in the country plant a large garden with many rows of vegetables?

_____

3. What type of garden might city dwellers plant? _____

_____

4. What type of garden might be planted by people with a small plot of land? _____

_____

B Write a definition for each word or phrase. Use a dictionary, if necessary.

1. preserved _____

2. out of season _____

3. topsoil _____

Review

A Write *Cereals*, *Grasses*, or *Vegetables* before each description.

_____ 1. These plants grow a portion of their stems underground.

_____ 2. Many plants called by this name are really fruits.

_____ 3. This general term describes plants grown for their edible seeds, or grains.

_____ 4. Examples of these grasses include barley and rye.

_____ 5. These plants have fibrous roots and inflorescences, or spikelets.

B Match the sentence parts by writing the letter on the line provided.

_____ 1. Oats

_____ 2. Wheat

_____ 3. Corn

_____ 4. Wild rice

_____ 5. Kenaf

_____ 6. Tomatoes

_____ 7. Wild vegetables

a. has kernels that grow on ears and are protected by husks.

b. is a promising new crop because its pulp can be used to make newsprint.

c. are eaten raw as well as made into paste, ketchup, and juice.

d. is used for making bread.

e. include onions and dandelion greens.

f. is expensive because it is not extensively grown in commercial quantities.

g. are grown as livestock feed and are also used in cereals.

C Complete the following sentences. Write your answers on the lines provided.

1. A _____ is an edible, dry fruit with a single seed and an attached hull.

2. Kenaf plants look like stalks of _____.

3. _____ may have been the first crop to have been domesticated and cultivated by humans.

4. Each ear of corn produces about 18 rows of _____.

5. Wild rice grows in _____ and along the shores of rivers and lakes.

6. Corn is called the _____ of grain crops in North America.

7. _____ and _____ are two crops that support much of the world's population.

8. Oats contain the greatest amount and best quality of _____ of all the cereal grains.

Herbs

Herbs actually include a wide variety of helpful but nonrelated plants. Herbs are particularly useful for cooking and for healing.

The best-known herbs are culinary, or the ones used for cooking. Because they add flavors to foods, herbs are often added to soups, salads, stews, and desserts. Generally speaking, herbs are plants grown for their leaves or stems. Parsley and oregano are herbs. Spices, on the other hand, are usually the seeds of plants that are used in cooking for their flavor. Pepper is a spice.

Herbs are also grown for their **medicinal** properties. Many plants contain chemicals, which are extracted, or removed, and used as medicines. Minor headaches and dizziness as well as serious or even life-threatening diseases have been treated with herbal remedies. In our country's colonial days, most families had an herb garden outside the kitchen door. There herbs to cure ills and herbs to make meals taste better were grown.

Like many herbs, chives can be grown in a kitchen window and then harvested as needed year-round.

Write the answers to the following questions.

1. What are herbs? _____

_____

2. For what two purposes are herbs grown? _____

_____

3. Which herbs are best known? _____

4. Which parts of the herb plant are eaten? _____

5. What is an example of an herb? _____

6. To what kinds of foods are herbs added? _____

_____

7. What is a spice? _____

_____

8. What is an example of a spice? _____

Venus's Flytraps

Venus's flytraps are unusual plants. They grow only in the wet **pinelands** and sandy bays of North and South Carolina. However, the strangeness of these plants comes not from their limited growing range but from what they like to eat. Venus's flytraps, like pitcher plants, are insect eaters.

These plants have short, horizontal underground stems called *rhizomes.* From the rhizomes grows a group of leaves that lie close to the ground. At the end of each leaf is a hinged section that opens and closes. Long spines, called *trigger hairs,* line the edge of each leaf half.

When an insect lands on the inside of a leaf, the two halves close. The trigger hairs mesh and lock the opening. Inside the leaf, the plant produces **acid** and **digestive juices** that kill and break down the insect. The dissolved insect parts are absorbed by the plant. Later, it opens its leaves again, and the inedible parts of the insect blow away in the wind.

Notice the trigger hairs on each hinged leaf section of this Venus's flytrap. These hairs can trap insects.

 Rewrite the following sentences. Put each group of words in correct order so that the words express a complete idea.

1. pinelands and sandy bays only Venus's flytraps grow of wet North and South Carolina in the

_____

_____

2. short, horizontal *rhizomes* called plants These have stems underground

_____

_____

3. ground a group From the grow close to leaves of that lie the rhizomes

_____

_____

4. plant digestive juices break insect down The acid and kill produces the and that

_____

_____

Purple Foxgloves

Purple foxgloves are annual, sometimes biennial, flowering plants. When they flower, they send up a tall stalk. On the top is a group of thimble-shaped white, pink, or lilac flowers.

Purple foxgloves are native to Europe, western Asia, and central Asia. They are grown in many countries around the world. These plants make a chemical called *digitalis*. Digitalis has been used for centuries as an important medicine for people with weak hearts.

At first, no one knew why purple foxglove extracts helped people. Then William Withering, an English doctor, studied the plant. In 1785, he published a pamphlet on how digitalis from purple foxglove could be used to cure dropsy. When a person's heart is too weak to pump blood through the body, fluids build up in the arms, legs, and stomach. This swelling was known as dropsy during Withering's time. He gave exact directions in his pamphlet on how to give digitalis to dropsy patients. When the digitalis helped the heart pump, the kidneys could flush excess fluids from the arms, legs, and stomach.

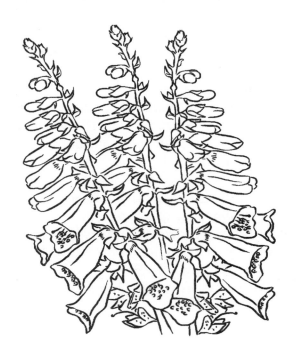

Many medicines come from various parts of plants. The purple foxglove makes a chemical called *digitalis*.

Today digitalis, which comes in a small pill, is prescribed by physicians. Many patients do not even realize that their heart medicine comes from the purple foxglove plant.

Read the following statements. If the statement is true, write *True* on the line provided. If the statement is not true, write *False*.

_____ 1. Purple foxglove is a perennial.

_____ 2. The plant sends up a tall stalk that holds its flowers.

_____ 3. Purple foxglove is native to the United States.

_____ 4. Purple foxglove makes a chemical called *digitalis.*

_____ 5. Digitalis is an important medicine for people with weak hearts.

_____ 6. William Withering discovered digitalis in 1982.

_____ 7. Digitalis prevents fluids from building up in the arms, legs, and stomach.

_____ 8. To get digitalis today, people must grow their own purple foxglove plants.

Centuries ago, sugarcane plants grew wild on islands in the South Pacific. After the demand for sweet foods grew, people began to cultivate the wild sugarcane plants. Today sugarcane is a domesticated plant.

Sugarcane is a tall member of the grass family. A sugarcane stalk has a pithy center. This is where the sugar is located. By harvest time, this pith can contain as much as 15 percent sugar. The sugar is formed when the plant photosynthesizes. But the plant does not use all of the sugar. It stores some of the sugar in the stalk.

In ancient India, sugarcane was grown as a crop. The Indians squeezed the plants in machines called *presses* and then boiled the liquid. After the liquid boiled away, a brown sugar was left. Today raising sugarcane is big business. Sugar is eaten in the largest amounts by Americans and Canadians.

Write the answers to the following questions.

1. Where did sugarcane grow wild? _____

_____

2. Is sugarcane a wild plant or a domesticated plant today? _____

_____

3. In what plant family is sugarcane? _____

_____

4. In what part of the sugarcane plant is sugar found? _____

_____

5. When is this sugar made in the plant? _____

_____

6. Where was sugarcane grown as a crop in the past? _____

_____

7. How was sugar produced there? _____

_____

8. Who eats the most sugar today? _____

_____

Tea Plants

Although there are many kinds of tea, most tea is harvested from two plant species: *Thea sinensis* and *Thea assamica*. The first species grows in southwest China, northeast India, and Cambodia. The second species grows in southeast Asia. These plants are shrubs and usually grow to be about 1 meter (3 feet) tall.

Shrubs grown for commercial tea production are started from seeds or **cuttings.** The plants are cut back so that many twigs will grow. These twigs produce small, tender leaves and one unopened leaf bud. The leaves and bud are picked and then combined to make tea.

The roots, leaves, twigs, and bark of many other plants can be soaked in hot water to make tea. For example, **mint, chamomile,** and **sassafras** make very good teas. Many people drink these teas because they do not contain caffeine. Caffeine, a chemical found in *Thea sinensis* and *Thea assamica*, causes the heart to beat faster.

Three different types of tea are produced: black, green, and oolong. Dark **black tea** is made from fermented leaves. **Green tea** is made from leaves that were not fermented before being dried. **Oolong tea** is made from leaves that were partly fermented before being dried. Commercial teas are blends of these three types. Some custom tea blends have been given the names of the people for whom they were originally blended; for example, Earl Grey and Queen Mary teas.

Complete the following sentences. Write your answers on the lines provided.

1. Tea is usually harvested from two different plant species: _____

   and _____.

2. Both plants are shrubs and usually grow to be about _____ tall.

3. Young shrubs grown for commercial tea production are started from

   _____ or _____.

4. The tea plant is cut back so that many _____ will grow.

5. When the twigs grow, they make small, tender _____ and one

   unopened _____.

6. _____, _____, and _____ are
   other plants that make very good teas.

7. Many people drink these teas because they do not contain _____.

8. The three different types of tea are _____, _____,

   and _____.

9. Commercial teas are _____ of the three types of tea.

10. _____ and _____ are custom tea blends.

Coffee Plants

Coffee trees or shrubs are related to the **gardenia** and **common bedstraw** plants. There are many species of coffee plants, but only two are grown for commercial use: *Coffea arabica* and *Coffea canephora*.

Coffee trees grow in tropical areas where abundant rain falls, such as Central America, South America, East Africa, and Java. The trees flower once or twice a year. Coffee beans are the plant's berries. Each berry has two seeds that are covered by an edible flesh and a red skin or pulp. The berries are picked by hand, washed, and dried. Then they are put through a machine that removes the pulp. Next, the beans are roasted. Roasting the beans makes their flavor stronger. Finally, a variety of beans are blended together to make the best cup of coffee.

A Read the following statements. If the statement is true, write *True* on the line provided. If the statement is not true, write *False*.

_____ 1. Coffee tree plants are related to marigolds.

_____ 2. Only two species of coffee trees exist.

_____ 3. Coffee trees grow in tropical areas.

_____ 4. Coffee trees are grown in Central America, South America, East Africa, and Java.

_____ 5. The coffee bean is the plant's seed.

_____ 6. The berry has three seeds.

_____ 7. The berry is covered by a red pulp.

_____ 8. The berries are machine picked.

_____ 9. A machine also removes their pulp.

_____ 10. Coffee beans are roasted.

_____ 11. Roasting weakens the flavor of the beans.

B Write the answers to the following questions. Use complete sentences.

1. To what two plants are coffee trees related?

_____

_____

2. What species of coffee tree plants are grown commercially?

_____

_____

Aloe Vera Plants

Aloe veras are succulents, plants that hold large amounts of water in their stems and leaves. Succulent plants are squishy to the touch. Aloe veras are in the same family as lilies, onions, and asparagus.

Aloe plants are mentioned in the Bible and have been considered **healing plants** for centuries. They thrived in the dry, hot climate of the Middle East. They are not native to the United States, but historians believe that the plants may have been brought to the Americas on Columbus's ships. Today aloe vera plants are grown in the dry climate of the southwestern United States.

These houseplants have long, spiky leaves. When a leaf is torn, a thick, clear fluid leaks out. This aloe juice has medicinal properties and is particularly helpful for burns. Rubbing the juice on minor burns stops the pain and helps the injured area heal quickly. Many people who have houseplants keep an aloe vera plant handy in case of burns.

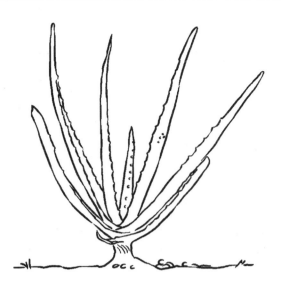

The aloe vera plant has medicinal and cosmetic uses.

Aloe juice is also used in skin products and cosmetics, or makeup. The aloe's fluid, a gel, goes into the skin and helps make it softer and smoother. Aloe gel is found in skin creams, body lotions, soap, shampoo, and makeup. Many people like aloe in their cosmetics because it is a natural product.

Write the answers to the following questions.

1. What is a succulent? _____

2. In what family are aloe veras included? _____

3. Are aloe veras native to the United States? _____

4. How did aloe veras come to the Americas? _____

5. In what book are aloes mentioned? _____

6. In what part of the United States are aloe plants grown? _____

7. What do the leaves of the aloe vera plant look like? _____

8. What medicinal use does aloe juice have? _____

9. How does aloe help skin? _____

10. What are five kinds of products that contain aloe? _____

_____

Raisins

Raisins are sun-dried grapes. Historians believe that long ago people learned to dry grapes so that the raisins could be stored and eaten during the winter months. Raisins were described in the writings of both the ancient Egyptians and Persians.

In the United States, grape plants whose grapes are used to make raisins are grown in California. They were introduced into this country by monks who established missions along the California coast in the sixteenth century. Commercial raisin production began in California in the 1870s. The most common grapes used for raisins are Thompson seedless grapes. This variety was introduced as cuttings from Turkey by William Thompson in 1872.

Grapes are harvested in August and September. They are dried outdoors until their water level drops to about 15 percent. Then they are placed in sweat boxes. Mild heat makes all the raisins have the same moisture content. The raisins are cleaned, **destemmed**, and inspected before being packed and sold.

A Write the answers to the following questions.

1. In whose writings were raisins first described? _____

_____

2. Where were raisins first produced commercially in the U.S.? _____

_____

3. What type of grape is most commonly used for raisins? _____

_____

B Review your knowledge of useful or odd plants. Match the sentence parts by writing the letter on the line provided.

_____ 1. Herbs

_____ 2. Venus's flytraps

_____ 3. Purple foxgloves

_____ 4. Sugarcane

_____ 5. With tea plants,

_____ 6. With coffee plants,

_____ 7. Aloe veras

_____ 8. Raisins

a. produce the medicine digitalis.

b. leaves and buds are picked and combined to make a drink.

c. are used for cooking and for medicinal properties.

d. are used in cosmetics and also as a medicine for burns.

e. is a tall member of the grass family.

f. are sun-dried grapes.

g. are insectivorous plants.

h. berries are dried, roasted, and blended to make a drink.

Maple Syrup and Sugar

Sugar maple trees grow primarily in the northeastern United States. These trees produce a sap that is used to make maple syrup and maple sugar. Native Americans were the first to collect and use the sap. They taught the European settlers how to turn the sap into syrup and sugar.

Sap is a mixture of sugar and water. On warm days following cold nights, the sap *runs,* or flows, through the trees. The warm days help the maple trees convert starch into sugar. Sugars and starches are similar **chemical molecules;** they are both carbohydrates. The trees make the sap as an energy source.

Maple sap is still collected today. For four to six weeks between January and April, the maple trees are cut, or tapped. Holes are drilled into the trees, and spouts are inserted. The sap drips out of the trees into buckets or plastic tubing. If the sap drips into buckets, it is collected by hand and brought to a sugarhouse. If the sap drips into plastic tubes, it is carried directly from the trees to the sugarhouse. There the sap is boiled in large tanks to make the water evaporate and to concentrate the sugar. When the sap is about 66 percent sugar, it becomes maple syrup. More water is evaporated to make maple sugar.

Maple syrup and sugar were important trade items until the late 1800s. Then sugar made from sugarcane became less expensive to use. Today Quebec, Canada, is the largest producer of maple syrup in the world. Vermont and New York are the largest producers in the United States.

A Match the sentence parts by writing the letter on the line provided.

_____ 1. Native Americans in the northeast	**a.** as an energy source for the trees.
_____ 2. Maple trees make sap	**b.** and taken to a sugarhouse.
_____ 3. When the tree is tapped,	**c.** to remove water and concentrate the sugar.
_____ 4. Sap is collected	**d.** taught settlers how to turn sap into syrup.
_____ 5. Maple sap is boiled	**e.** sap flows into buckets or tubes.

B Complete the following sentences. Write your answers on the lines provided.

1. Sugar maples grow mostly in the _____ United States.

2. Sap is collected for _____ weeks in early spring.

3. Maple syrup is about _____ percent sugar.

4. _____ is the world's largest producer of maple syrup.

5. The largest maple syrup producers in the U.S. are _____ and

   _____.

Paper

Using wood from trees to produce paper has a long history. In 1719, a French scientist and inventor, Rene de Reaumer, wrote a report about using wood to produce paper. He got this idea when he examined wasps' nests and saw bits of wood in the paperlike nests. By 1841, the first factory using ground wood to make paper had been built in Nova Scotia, Canada. In 1870, the *New York Times* was the first newspaper to use newsprint made from wood.

Ground-wood paper pulp is made from the whole or broken xylem vessels and fibers. These xylem cells are composed of cellulose—a chemical very similar to starch. The other component of xylem vessels is lignin. It is an undesirable compound for making paper because it is brownish in color. Several methods were invented to remove lignin from wood pulp and leave only the cellulose.

Today North America is the largest producer and **consumer** of paper. Most of the paper produced in the United States is made from yellow pines and aspens that grow in the southern and western states.

Unfortunately, making paper from trees causes problems. Clearing large areas of trees can cause erosion because nothing is left to hold the soil in place. Also, the chemicals used to produce wood pulp have been dumped into **waterways.** These chemicals are poisonous to plants, animals, and people.

Read the following statements. If the statement is true, write *True* on the line provided. If the statement is not true, write *False.*

_____ 1. Rene de Reaumer wrote a report about using wood to produce paper in 1819.

_____ 2. He got this idea from examining wasps' nests.

_____ 3. The first factory for making wood-pulp paper was built in Nova Scotia, Canada.

_____ 4. The *New York Times* was the first newspaper to use newsprint made from wood.

_____ 5. Cellulose and lignin are needed in the wood pulp to make paper.

_____ 6. Most paper produced in the U.S. is made from yellow pines and aspens from the South and West.

_____ 7. The chemicals used in the making of paper are poisonous.

_____ 8. Clearing trees from large areas has no effect on the soil.

Cotton

Cotton plants are native to tropical areas, where they grow as perennials. In the southern United States, cotton plants are grown as annuals because the winters are too cold for them to survive.

Cotton is a self-pollinating as well as a bee-pollinating plant. After a plant is fertilized, it develops a large fruit. This cotton boll contains many seeds. When the boll is fully mature, it splits open, and the cotton fibers expand. The cotton plant looks as though it is covered with white snowballs. Cotton fibers are made of cellulose, a very strong and durable fiber used to make items such as clothing and canvas.

Not only the cotton fibers but also the cotton seeds are valuable. These seeds contain about 35 percent oil. The oil is removed by squeezing the seeds under high pressure. A cake of seeds remains. The seed cake, without its oil, is an excellent feed for livestock.

These Mississippi plants show bolls and fluffy cotton.

■ Write the answers to the following questions.

1. Where are cotton plants native? _____

2. Are cotton plants grown as annuals or perennials in the United States? _____

3. By what two methods can cotton plants be pollinated? _____

_____

4. What is the fruit of a cotton plant called? _____

5. What happens when the boll matures? _____

_____

6. What are cotton fibers made of? _____

7. What is done with the cotton seeds? _____

_____

8. How much oil do cotton seeds contain? _____

Rubber

Lesson 4

Christopher Columbus found rubber plants in the tropical areas of the Americas. He brought the plants back to Europe, where they were given the name *rubber* after being used to rub out or erase pencil marks. Europeans did not think that rubber plants were particularly useful or pretty. Only many years later would the product of rubber trees be used commercially.

Natural rubber is obtained from *Hevea brasiliensis,* a kind of tree that grows naturally in the Amazon basin in Brazil. This tree produces a thick, white liquid called *latex.* This latex contains water, resins, proteins, sugars, and 30 to 40 percent rubber. Latex is made by the trees in their latex vessels, which connect with their phloem vessels. The trees are tapped several times a week during the growing season. A single tree can produce rubber for 30 years.

Latex is collected and mixed with **acetic acid**, which coagulates, or thickens, the rubber. The rubber is dried, mixed with coloring, and then added to sulfur and **lead oxide.** The resulting mixture is heated. Used rubber is also added and mixed in. Rubber is used in many products—such as tires, elastic, rubber bands, and toys—that are important in our world today. Ninety percent of the natural rubber used today comes from Asia.

Complete the following sentences. Write your answers on the lines provided.

1. _____ found rubber plants in the _____ areas of the Americas.

2. In _____, rubber was named after being used to erase pencil marks.

3. Europeans did not think that rubber plants were very _____ or _____.

4. Rubber trees grow naturally in the _____ basin in Brazil.

5. These trees produce a thick, white liquid called _____.

6. The latex contains _____ percent rubber.

7. One rubber tree can produce rubber for _____ years.

8. The latex is collected and mixed with _____ to coagulate the rubber.

9. The rubber is then _____, mixed with _____, and added to sulfur and lead oxide.

10. _____ is also added and mixed in.

11. Rubber is used in _____ and _____.

12. Today most natural rubber comes from _____.

Chocolate

Chocolate, a product of the cacao plant, was a sacred delicacy to the Aztecs of Mexico. Spanish explorers tried and liked the Aztec drink made of *chocolātl,* a drink similar to today's hot chocolate. The drink became popular in Europe, and the Spanish government started to harvest cocoa from plantations that they set up in Mexico.

A dozen countries produce cocoa today. Cacao plants need a warm, humid climate; fertile soil; and extensive cultivation to grow. The plant produces leaves, flowers, and fruit. The ripe fruit, or pod, contains cacao beans. (The cacao beans became known as cocoa beans in English-speaking countries because of a spelling error by importers.) Each pod has 20 to 40 bean-shaped seeds. They are harvested from the pods and dried in the sun. After drying and cleaning, the beans are roasted. The beans look, smell, and taste like chocolate after they have been roasted. North Americans are the major consumers of chocolate today. Chocolate is used in many products, including drinks, cake mixes, candies, and syrup.

The broken pod shows the seeds from which chocolate is made.

Read the following statements. If the statement is true, write *True* on the line provided. If the statement is not true, write *False.*

_____ 1. Chocolate was a delicacy to the Aztecs of Mexico.

_____ 2. Spanish explorers liked the Aztec chocolate drink.

_____ 3. The drink became popular in Africa.

_____ 4. The Spanish set up cocoa plantations in Mexico.

_____ 5. Two dozen countries produce chocolate today.

_____ 6. Cacao plants need cold, dry climates in order to grow.

_____ 7. Cocoa (cacao) beans are berries that grow in pods.

_____ 8. After drying and cleaning, the beans are roasted.

_____ 9. South Americans consume the most chocolate.

_____ 10. Chocolate is made from the leaves of the cacao plant.

Corn Products

UNIT 9

Corn has long been grown as food for both animals and people. Originally, animals ate chopped corn plants and kernels off the cob, while humans ate only corn kernels. Native Americans grew corn and taught early colonists about the plants.

Since that time, people have discovered how to use corn plants in many other ways. Many products—such as corn oil, sugars, starches, alcohols, and corn syrup—are now made from these plants.

Corn oil is a healthier oil to eat than many other oils. Because it is an unsaturated fat, corn oil does not contain many **hydrogen atoms.** It stays a liquid when it is chilled. Saturated fats, on the other hand, take a solid form when they are chilled. Butter, for example, is a saturated fat. Doctors have learned that high cholesterol levels can be found in the bodies of people who have a diet rich in saturated fats. High cholesterol levels are one cause of heart attacks. Doctors recommend that patients replace saturated fats in their diets with vegetable oils. Unsaturated corn oil, therefore, is one choice for people with heart problems and others concerned about their health.

Corn sugar is another product made from corn. When corn kernels are soaked in weak acid and then ground, starch is released. This starch is a starting material for many other corn products. It is treated with enzymes and turned into sugars. Corn sugars now compete with beet and cane sugars on the sugar market.

In addition, corn starch and sugar can be fermented by yeast and bacteria to produce **ethyl alcohol.** This alcohol can be used to make a form of gasoline. The alcohol-containing gas is called *gasohol,* and an unleaded version is called *ethanol.* The world has a limited supply of petroleum. It is hoped that this fuel mixture will help conserve petroleum.

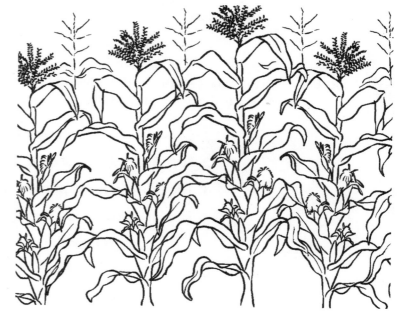

Corn syrup is produced from starch, too. High-fructose corn syrup is a liquid that contains a large amount of the sugar fructose. High-fructose corn syrup is used as an inexpensive sweetener for juices and soft drinks.

Corn is no longer just a food for animals and humans. Many products are now made from this plant. Even more uses for corn may be discovered in the future.

A Write the definitions of the words. Use a dictionary, if necessary.

1. saturated _____

2. enzyme _____

3. cob _____

4. gasoline _____

5. unsaturated _____

B Write the answers to the following questions. Use complete sentences.

1. What corn products are described in the text on page 80? _____

_____

_____

2. What corn product is added to juices and soft drinks? Why? _____

_____

_____

3. How can corn help conserve petroleum? _____

_____

_____

_____

4. Why is corn oil a healthier oil to eat than many other oils? _____

_____

_____

_____

5. How does use of corn today compare with use of corn in the past? _____

_____

_____

_____

UNIT 9

Many plant products can be fermented. This process mixes a plant product with organisms such as yeast. These organisms break the plant down and produce the gas carbon dioxide as well as ethyl alcohol.

Soy sauce, for example, is a fermented product. Soy beans are boiled until they are soft. This soy mixture is added to roasted and ground wheat. A fungus is added to the mixture along with salt. Finally, to become soy sauce, the mixture is allowed to ferment for almost a year.

Perhaps the best-known fermented foods are wine and spirits, or hard liquors. Once orchards were established, the settlers began to ferment fruit. Apples were made into hard cider. **Elderberries,** currants, and wild grapes were fermented into wine. In fermentation, yeast feeds on the sugars in the fruit and produces ethyl alcohol. The fermentation stops when the amount of alcohol reaches 15 to 18 percent. This concentration inactivates the yeast.

Spirits were also made by the colonists in the Americas. They made beer from the corn given to them by Native Americans. They used plants they had grown for food to make beer as well. Beer was made from pumpkins, potatoes, plums, carrots, and turnips. By the mid-1640s, a **distilling apparatus** had been invented. With this equipment, liquors such as brandies and rye could be made from fermented fruits and rye grains.

A Write the answers to the following questions.

1. What organisms are used to bring about fermentation? _____

2. What is added to soy beans to make soy sauce? _____

   _____

3. What three fruits were used by the colonists to make wine?_____

   _____

4. What six plants were used by the colonists to make beer? _____

   _____

B Review your knowledge of plant products. Think of products made from each of the following plants or plant parts. Write your answers on your own paper.

1. two from maple sap
2. three from cotton
3. two from wood pulp
4. four from rubber
5. four from chocolate
6. six from fermented foods
7. five from corn

Apple Varieties

Farmers used to plant varieties of apples that are now called *antique.* Technically, an antique is something that is at least one hundred years old. In this case, the word *antique* has a different meaning. During the 1800s, people grew a large variety of apples. Most people living in the country had at least one apple tree. Some of these older varieties of apples were called Northern Spy, Baldwin, and Winesap.

A McIntosh apple is best for eating. Other varieties are better for cooking, drying, or making cider.

Few supermarkets today carry antique varieties of apples. Instead, they sell Red Delicious, Golden Delicious, and McIntosh apples. Today growing only a few varieties of apples makes sense. They all come into season at the same time, which makes harvesting simple. These apples store well and look good for long periods of time. The antique varieties were not always red or perfectly shaped. Many people want apples that look and taste like the Delicious and McIntosh varieties.

Antique varieties may not store well and may not be as pretty as modern varieties. However, antique apple growers say that their apples are better tasting and just too good to abandon. Small-orchard owners sometimes grow older varieties and sell them at roadside stands or at produce markets in cities. These orchard owners insist that our great-grandparents knew something that most people today are missing out on: the taste and flavor of apples with quaint names like Black Gilliflower and Westfield Seek-No-Further.

▪ Write the answers to the following questions.

1. What makes an apple variety antique? _____

_____

2. What are five antique varieties of apples? _____

_____

3. What are three newer apple varieties sold today? _____

_____

4. Who sells the antique varieties? _____

_____

5. Where are the antique varieties sold? _____

_____

Plants help prevent floods and often do a better job of it than dams made by people. Soil is able to absorb large amounts of water. Plant roots help keep soil in place. Often an area floods because of rain runoff. The rainwater comes off hillsides during a heavy rainstorm and can cause flooding in valleys. Engineers know that deforestation, or the removal of forests from hillsides, is the main reason for lowland floods. When no trees hold the soil in place, both rainwater and soil pour off the hills. Trees and other plants not only look good on hillsides but also act as natural dams.

In addition to floods, forest fires can destroy hectares (acres) of wooded land almost overnight. During a dry season, forest fires can be started in several ways. Lightning can strike a dead tree. Careless campers may leave campfires burning. Without thinking, some people throw cigarette butts out of their car window as they drive past a forest. The Forest Service tries to educate people to protect the forests in the national parks, but many fires still occur every year. The symbol of Smokey the Bear is a reminder to campers that forest fires are usually started by people. Many damaging fires can also be prevented by people.

Damaging fires and deforestation leave nothing to hold soil in place. Lowland floods can result.

Complete the following sentences. Write your answers on the lines provided.

1. _____ help prevent floods and often do a better job than dams.

2. _____ is able to absorb large amounts of water.

3. Plant _____ help keep the soil in place.

4. Floods often occur because of rain _____.

5. _____ and _____ pour off hills when no trees hold the soil in place.

6. _____ and _____ not only look good on hillsides but also act as natural dams.

7. Forest fires are often caused by _____ campers who leave fires burning.

8. During a dry season, fires can also be started by _____.

9. Forest fires are often started by _____ and can be prevented by _____.

Saving the Topsoil

The United States has always been known as a leader in the field of agriculture. Our midwestern and western states produce large amounts of the world's wheat, corn, and other crops. However, if it were not for the dust bowl of the 1930s, the U.S. might not have become as agriculturally rich as it is today.

When farmers settled the western states, they knew or cared little about using the proper procedures for growing crops. Land was abused. The topsoil was loosened so that plant seeds could be easily **sown.** Farmers plowed straight rows and did not leave trees to break the wind. The loosened soil would blow away on windy days. The western states are semiarid; they do not get much rain. Some years went by when no rain fell at all. Underground streams, called *aquifers,* dried up. The soil could no longer be kept moist. The land became like a desert. By the 1930s, dust storms were occurring by the hundreds. Wheat and other crops could not grow in this dry soil.

Improper farming techniques and overharvesting of trees and other vegetation cause loss of topsoil.

In the 1930s, botanists and soil scientists from the Department of Agriculture tried to restore America's croplands. They introduced proper water conservation practices and suggested new ways to till the soil. Contour plowing and the planting of windbreaks prevented valuable topsoil from blowing away. New crops were planted to help hold the soil in place. Such practices are still being used today to prevent the possibility of another dust bowl.

Read the following statements. If the statement is true, write *True* on the line provided. If the statement is not true, write *False*.

_____ 1. The United States has never been known as a leader in agriculture.

_____ 2. The southern states have produced much of the world's wheat and corn.

_____ 3. Early farmers knew little about the proper procedures for growing crops.

_____ 4. When no rain fell, underground streams called *aquifers* dried up.

_____ 5. Dust storms by the hundreds occurred during the 1920s.

_____ 6. In the 1930s, botanists and soil scientists tried to restore America's croplands.

Tropical Rain Forests

Tropical rain forests of the world are found in areas near the earth's equator. This imaginary line runs around the middle of the earth and separates the Northern and Southern hemispheres.

Tropics are lush, green areas with thickly wooded forests. Many exotic and colorful plants, such as banana and pineapple plants, grow in the tropics. Because these lands are densely covered with so many kinds of plants, many people think that they are fertile areas. However, tropical soils are not fertile. Tree and plant growth is supported by the great amount of rain that falls each year. The tropics get five to ten times the amount of rainfall that nontropical areas receive. Unfortunately, this great amount of rain leaches nutrients from the soil. They are washed out of the soil by the rain and carried into nearby waterways.

Another problem in the tropics is the loss of the rain forests. When tropical areas are deforested, the thin, fragile soil erodes and washes away into rivers and streams. The remaining dry soil becomes hard like clay when it is exposed to the sun. Crops cannot grow in such soil. In addition, people destroy the rain forests. Large trees provide valuable lumber. Rain forests in Brazil and other countries are being chopped down so that food crops can be grown. However, tropical rain forests help put oxygen into the atmosphere. Such rain forests are not good areas to exploit because they cannot be replaced.

Notice how each of the following words is used in the text. Then write a definition next to each word. Use a dictionary, if necessary.

1. hemisphere _____

_____

2. exotic _____

_____

3. fertile _____

_____

4. leach _____

_____

5. deforested _____

_____

6. exploit _____

_____

Pollution

Pollution of the soil comes in many forms. One type of soil pollution comes from the toxic wastes made by industries. Soil pollution also comes from fertilizers and **pesticides** that are used to help grow agricultural crops. Such chemicals can remain in the soil for a long time.

Salt, or sodium chloride, causes another kind of soil pollution. Salt is not considered a pollutant when it is on the dinner table. However, it is one of the most common pollutants worldwide. Sodium chloride and other salts are concentrated in irrigation water. When fields are semiarid, farmers dig **furrows.** They then irrigate by channeling river water to fill the furrows and keep the soil moist for plants. This river water brings with it dissolved salts. Unfortunately, as the water evaporates, it leaves the salts behind.

High levels of salts prevent plants from growing. More salts are added from fertilizers that run off the fields and into waterways. These salts, too, are left behind during irrigation. Making an area too salty for plant growth is called *salinization.* Because it ruins farmland, salinization is a particularly dangerous form of soil pollution.

A Rewrite the following sentences. Put each group of words in correct order so that the words express a complete idea.

1. pollution industries the toxic wastes made by Some comes from

   _____

2. sodium chloride, most common of the worldwide pollutants is one Salt, or

   _____

3. channeled River into fields the to fill furrows plants moist keep and water is to

   _____

4. water dissolved salts The river brings it with

   _____

5. salts prevent growing High plants from levels of

   _____

B Write the answers to the following questions. Use your own paper.

1. What is one example of environmental pollution that you have seen?

2. What do you think was the cause of this particular pollution?

3. What do you think can be done to fight such pollution of the environment?

U
N
I
T

10

Plants and insects have been close associates for millions of years. They need each other. Most plants produce flowers, which attract insects. Flies, ants, and beetles feed on flowers. They actually eat the blossoms. They also help pollinate the plants.

Some flowers attract bees. Bees are well-known for their interest in flower **nectar** and pollen. They make the nectar into honey, and the pollen into bee bread. As a bee flies from one plant to the next, it takes pollen with it. Pollen from one plant is therefore carried to another plant. The bee is pollinating the second plant so that it can produce fruit and seeds. Other flowers attract beetles. They feed on the nectar, pick up pollen, and carry it to another plant. Magnolias, dogwood, peonies, and water lilies are pollinated in this way.

The yucca plant and the Pronuba moth have a long-standing relationship. The yucca plant, which grows in the southwestern United States, needs the Pronuba moth to grow its seeds. The Pronuba moth needs the yucca plant in order to hatch its eggs and raise its young. The yucca plant grows a stalk with a cluster of creamy white blossoms. The flowers' seed-making parts begin to develop before the blossoms open. The pistil grows long. The ovary becomes fatter, and the ovules become ready for fertilization. The stamens also grow outward, and the pollen ripens on the stamen tips. The petals unfold. At this point, the moths see the opened blossoms and fly into the flowers. Under the Pronuba's chin are curved arms called *palpi*. With the palpi, the Pronuba scrapes up pollen and forms it into a ball. Then the moth flies to the next blossom where it lays four or five eggs in the plant's ovary. It pushes the ball of pollen into the blossom's stigma. The plant is fertilized, and the eggs will hatch into **caterpillars**, which will later become adult moths. Without each other, neither the yucca nor the Pronuba moth would be able to survive.

■ Read the following statements. If the statement is true, write *True* on the line provided. If the statement is not true, write *False*.

_____ 1. Where there are many plants, insects will not live.

_____ 2. Most plants do not produce flowers.

_____ 3. Flowers attract insects.

_____ 4. Flies, ants, and beetles eat flower blossoms.

_____ 5. Bees like only the nectar of the flower.

_____ 6. Nectar is made into bee bread, and pollen is made into honey.

_____ 7. As a bee flies from one plant to the next, it takes pollen with it.

_____ 8. The yucca plant needs the Pronuba moth to grow its seeds.

Historically, new plant varieties were made by classical breeding techniques. Most crop plants were made in this way. For instance, a wheat variety that made many wheat kernels was fertilized with the pollen of a wheat variety that was very hardy. The offspring of these two plants would have both of these desirable traits. Today, however, plant scientists are producing new and better crop plants in the laboratory as well as in the fields. Genetic engineering is a new way to produce different varieties of plants.

Genetic materials, called *genes,* are found in the nucleus of every cell in a plant. One way to genetically engineer a plant is to perform a protoplast fusion. A plant is taken to a laboratory where it is ground up. It is no longer a whole plant but individual cells in a liquid mixture of nutrients. This mixture is called a *plant tissue culture.* It is much easier to genetically engineer single cells than a whole plant. A genetically engineered cell can later grow into a whole plant.

For example, a scientist might want to improve a plant by making it salt-tolerant. This improved plant could grow in areas where the groundwater contains higher than normal amounts of salt. The salt-tolerant plant would not wilt or die as other plants would in such a salty environment. The scientist might know of a plant that is salt-tolerant and would want to transfer the genes for salt tolerance from the plant that has them to the plant that does not.

First, a tissue culture is made from both plants. A small amount of tissue culture from these plants is transferred to a separate flask. Here the plant cell walls are removed. The cell walls normally protect plant cells from drying out and are also responsible for the stiffness of plant stems. The wall-less cells are called *protoplasts.* These cells are very fragile because they no longer have their walls for protection.

Next, the protoplasts from the two plants are joined together in pairs using a chemical. This joining step is called *protoplast fusion.* Many of these pairs are made during a protoplast fusion experiment. The fused protoplasts become one new large cell.

The genes in each of these cells are mixed together. Similar genes are discarded by the fused cell. Only one copy of each different gene is needed. The genes that are not found in both of the protoplasts are kept by the fused large cell. In this particular experiment, the single set of salt-tolerant genes would be kept by the fused protoplasts.

From a single fused cell, a whole plant can now be made to grow. Once the new plant has been grown, it is then tested for salt tolerance. If the plant proves to be salt tolerant, then it is, in fact, a new variety of plant that has been genetically engineered. From such genetic engineering of cells, scientists are able to develop new plants with desirable traits.

A Complete the following sentences. Write your answers on the lines provided.

1. In the past, _____ techniques were used to develop new varieties of plants.

2. _____ is the modern method now used.

3. _____ contains plant cells in a liquid mixture of nutrients.

4. _____ are plant cells whose walls have been removed.

B Review your knowledge of plants and the environment. Write the answers to the following questions. Use complete sentences.

1. What advantages do modern apple varieties have over antique ones? _____

_____

2. How do droughts contribute to forest fires? _____

_____

3. What did farmers learn from the dust bowl of the 1930s?

_____

4. Why are tropical rain forests so important? _____

_____

5. Why is salinization considered a form of soil pollution? _____

_____

6. Why do many plants need insects? _____

_____

7. What is one way genetic engineering is different from classical breeding techniques?

_____

_____

_____

End-of-Book Test

A Underline the word that correctly completes each sentence.

1. Bacteria used to be called (spirella, plants, animals).

2. A plant cell is made up of many parts called (genes, nuclei, organelles).

3. Chlorophyll makes plants look (orange, silver, green).

4. The top of the stigma feels (sticky, soft, stiff).

5. Cherries, plums, and peaches are (grains, drupes, seeds).

6. There are (few, several, many) varieties of apples.

7. Walnuts are grown for eating and for the (shells, leaves, oil) they produce.

8. Wheat, rice, and oats are (cereals, veins, vegetables).

9. The juice of the aloe vera plant can be used for (seasoning, burns, cuttings).

10. Raisins are sun-dried (prunes, gooseberries, grapes).

11. (Roots, Stems, Leaves) hold plants in place.

12. Sexual reproduction in plants requires a (spore, sperm, yeast) and an egg.

13. A (moss, fern, lichen) is made up of an alga and a fungus.

14. Dicots have (two, three, four) seed leaves.

15. Rubber trees produce a liquid called (acid, latex, water).

B Match the sentence parts by writing the letter on the line provided.

_____ 1. Sugarcane is   **a.** put oxygen into the atmosphere.

_____ 2. Maple trees make sap   **b.** a delicacy of the Aztecs.

_____ 3. Chocolate was   **c.** known for their medicinal properties.

_____ 4. The Pronuba moth helps   **d.** cause lowland floods.

_____ 5. Herbs are   **e.** a tall member of the grass family.

_____ 6. Spices are   **f.** grow for many years.

_____ 7. Deforestation can   **g.** are called *aquifers.*

_____ 8. Underground streams   **h.** as an energy source for the tree.

_____ 9. Rain forests help   **i.** seeds used for flavoring.

_____ 10. Perennial plants can   **j.** pollinate the yucca plant.

C Classify each plant or organism by writing its name under the correct heading.

1. pine   rose   cactus   spruce
    corn   oak   fir   sequoia

Gymnosperms   **Angiosperms**

a. _____   e. _____

b. _____   f. _____

c. _____   g. _____

d. _____   h. _____

2. apple   tomato   corn   cherry
    broccoli   carrot   pear   lettuce

Fruits   **Vegetables**

a. _____   e. _____

b. _____   f. _____

c. _____   g. _____

d. _____   h. _____

3. alga   fern   fungus   maple
    moss   lichen   marigold   hibiscus

Nonvascular Organisms   **Vascular Plants**

a. _____   e. _____

b. _____   f. _____

c. _____   g. _____

d. _____   h. _____

D Read each definition. Write the letter of the word by its definition.

a. dormant	**g.** digest	**m.** transplant
b. rhizome	**h.** delicacy	**n.** sow
c. prune	**i.** ornamental	**o.** edible
d. flagellum	**j.** annual	**p.** succulent
e. pesticides	**k.** temperate	**q.** medicinal
f. phloem	**l.** spore	**r.** decompose

_____ **1.** a plant that lives or grows for only one season

_____ **2.** a horizontal underground stem

_____ **3.** to scatter seeds so that they will grow into new plants

_____ **4.** a plant with stems and leaves that are able to hold water

_____ **5.** to shape a plant by cutting and trimming the leaves and branches

_____ **6.** to break down to absorb food

_____ **7.** able to be eaten

_____ **8.** in a resting condition

_____ **9.** a food that is special, tasty, and often rare and expensive

_____ **10.** describing plants grown for their beauty

_____ **11.** to remove and replant a growing plant

_____ **12.** capable of being used as medicine

_____ **13.** chemicals used to kill harmful insects or pests

_____ **14.** describing a climate that is neither very cold nor very hot

_____ **15.** a whiplike appendage on microorganisms that helps them move

_____ **16.** a small, seedlike reproductive cell in ferns, fungi, and mosses

_____ **17.** to rot and decay

_____ **18.** a plant's vascular tissue that carries food

Glossary

A

acetic acid: a colorless organic solvent used in the manufacture of rubber

acid: any of a large class of chemicals with a pH level below 7 (neutral) and with a biting, sour taste

altitude: the height of something; it is usually above a level used for reference, such as sea level

angiosperms: a class of plants that have seeds enclosed in an ovary

annual: a plant that lives and grows for only one season

antheridium: the male part of mosses; it contains sperm

archegonium: the female part of mosses; it produces a single egg

arctic: in the geographical area of the world that includes the North Pole

B

bacilli: bacteria with long, round-ended shapes

bed: a small area used for growing plants

biennial: a plant that lives and grows for only two seasons

black tea: a dark tea made with leaves that have been fermented

bog: a swampland or marsh

C

cambium: a growing layer of cells in a tree's trunk; it produces the xylem and phloem. This layer also shows the growth rings of the tree.

chamomile: a plant, native to Europe and Asia, with small, white flowers and fine leaves. Dried chamomile is used for tea.

carbon dioxide: a colorless, odorless gas produced by animal respiration

caterpillar: the long, wormlike larva of moths and butterflies

chemical molecule: the simplest part of a substance; a molecule contains one or more atoms

chloroplast: an area within a cell where chlorophyll is found and where photosynthesis takes place

climate: the temperature, wind, and weather in a region over a period of time

cocci: bacteria with round shapes

commercially: producing for sale in a market

common bedstraw: a plant with whorled leaves, small, white or yellow flowers, and prickly burrs

consumer: a buyer of items offered for sale

culinary: related to the kitchen and cooking

cultivate: to prepare or improve land by fertilizing and plowing for the raising of crops

currants: prickly shrubs that produce black, greenish, or red fruit

cuttings: twigs or pieces of a plant taken to form new roots and then to be planted

D

decompose: to rot and decay

delicacy: a food that is special, tasty, and sometimes rare and expensive

destemmed: a term used to describe fruit that has had its stem removed

dicots: one of the two divisions in the angiosperm group of plants; dicots have a paired seed leaf

digest: to break down and absorb food

digestive juices: the chemicals in a person's, an animal's, or a plant's digestive system that break down foods

distilling apparatus: equipment used to produce alcohol

diverse: composed of many distinct elements or qualities

domesticated: cared for by humans rather than growing in the wild

dormant: in a resting condition

dwarf: a plant that is smaller than normal size when mature

E

edible: able to be eaten

elderberries: small fruit produced by an elder tree; elderberries are often used to make wine

ethyl alcohol: a chemical that is produced by the fermentation of sugar and starches

F

fir: an evergreen tree that has flat needles

flagellum: a whiplike appendage on *euglena* that helps them move

furrow: a narrow trench made in the ground by a plow

G

gardenia: a shrub, native to China, that has glossy leaves and large, white flowers

gooseberries: shrubs, native to Europe and Asia, that have greenish flowers and edible greenish berries

green tea: a tea that is made from green leaves that were not fermented before being dried

growth ring: the growth of the cambium layer in a tree trunk during one year's time

gymnosperms: members of the pine family; their seeds are not enclosed in an ovary but exposed in a cone

H

healing plant: an herb that can be used to cure illnesses

hedges: bushes that are grown together to form a plant wall

hemlock: an evergreen tree that has flat needles and small cones

hemp: an Asian plant that has fibrous stems used to make cords; also called kenaf

hothouse plants: plants grown in temperature-regulated greenhouses rather than outdoors

hydrogen atoms: particles of hydrogen, a chemical element and the lightest of all gases

I

inherit: to get or receive the traits or properties of someone or something else

insectivorous: feeding on insects; for example, a pitcher plant

J

Jerusalem artichoke tubers: plants that grow as tubers, or short, underground fleshy stems; they are eaten as vegetables

joint: the area where two parts are connected

K

killing frost: the freezing temperature that causes a frost and kills off annual plants

L

lead oxide: a chemical compound made up of lead and oxygen

lobes: the extensions or projections of a leaf that give it a unique shape

M

mature: fully grown

medicinal: capable of being used as medicine; medicinal plants can be used to cure illnesses

Mediterranean countries: lands that border the Mediterranean Sea

mint: a plant cultivated for its fragrant leaves

monocots: one of the two divisions in the angiosperm group of plants; monocots have a single seed leaf

N

native: originating from a certain area or country

nectar: a sweet liquid produced by some flowers to attract bees and therefore bring about pollination

node: the point on a plant stem where a leaf or bud is attached

nutrients: nourishing ingredients in plants or other foods that are needed to keep something else alive

nutritious: providing nutrients necessary for growth and survival

O

offspring: the products that come from asexual or sexual reproduction

okra: a plant that grows in temperate and tropical areas and has edible green pods

oolong tea: a dark tea that is partly fermented before being dried

organelle: a part of a cell that has a specific function

ornamental: describing plants that are grown for their beauty

ovary: a part of a pistil on a flower; it contains the ovules

P

parasite: a living organism that lives off of another living organism

perennial: a plant that lives for several years or longer

pesticides: chemicals used to kill harmful insects or pests

phloem: a plant's vascular tissue that carries food

photosynthesis: the plant process that uses energy from the sun to produce sugar, or food, for the plant

pinelands: areas where certain types of pine trees grow

pith: the soft, spongy tissue in the middle of plant stems and branches

prune: to shape a plant by cutting and trimming the leaves and branches

R

rhizome: a horizontal underground stem

rootstocks: rhizomes, or horizontal stems

S

saprophyte: a fungus or bacterium that lives on dead matter

sassafras: a North American tree whose roots can be brewed to make tea

seed leaf: the part of a plant's seed that becomes a leaf as the plant grows. Monocots have one seed leaf; dicots have two.

sow: to scatter seeds so that they will grow into new plants

spirilla: bacteria with spiral shapes

spore: the asexual, reproductive cell of ferns, fungi, and mosses

succulent: a plant with stems and leaves that are able to hold water; for example, a cactus or an aloe vera

swampland: a lowland area that contains much water; a marsh or a bog

symbiotic: living together in a mutually beneficial relationship

T

temperate: describing a climate that is neither very cold nor very hot

tilled: a term used to describe land that has been fertilized and plowed for planting

timber: trees that are cut down and used as a source of wood for plywood, furniture, house lumber, and so on

transplant: to remove and replant a growing plant

tumbleweeds: plants that grow in the western prairies of the United States; when dry, these plants break off and are rolled by the wind

V

vascular tissue: the xylem and phloem cells in a plant that bring water and minerals into the plant and also carry food to other parts of the plant

vibrios: bacteria with branched shapes

W

waterways: rivers or streams

whorl: an area on *Equisetum* that is curled in appearance

woody plant: a plant that has stems covered by bark

X

xylem: part of a plant's vascular system that carries water and minerals into and throughout the plant